EMPOWERMENT AND DEMOCRACY IN THE WORKPLACE

EMPOWERMENT AND DEMOCRACY IN THE WORKPLACE

Applying Adult Education Theory and Practice for Cultivating Empowerment

JOHN R. DEW

QUORUM BOOKS
Westport, Connecticut • London

Library of Congress Cataloging-in-Publication Data

Dew, John R.
    Empowerment and democracy in the workplace : applying adult
education theory and practice for cultivating empowerment / by John
R. Dew.
        p.   cm.
    Includes bibliographical references and index.
    ISBN 1–56720–094–X (alk. paper)
    1. Employee empowerment.   2. Democracy.   I. Title.
HD50.5.D49   1997
658.3′14—dc20   96–17926

British Library Cataloguing in Publication Data is available.

Library of Congress Catalog Card Number: 96–17926
ISBN: 1–56720–094–X

First published in 1997

Quorum Books, 88 Post Road West, Westport, CT 06881
An imprint of Greenwood Publishing Group, Inc.

Printed in the United States of America

The paper used in this book complies with the
Permanent Paper Standard issued by the National
Information Standards Organization (Z39.48–1984).

10 9 8 7 6 5 4 3 2 1

Contents

Introduction

This book is written from the perspective of the experiences of an adult education practitioner engaged in helping create empowering work systems in manufacturing, service organizations, city governments, and within educational systems.

There are many principles and practices from the adult education field that will help organizations effectively achieve an empowering and democratic condition in the workplace. The field of emancipatory education with its emphasis on praxis, reflective thinking, conscientization, and participatory research provides the key ingredient to generating change that will create an empowering workplace.

One of the guiding principles of this book is the concept of praxis. Praxis is a term that describes the process in which we consider our actions and refine those actions based on our understanding of what we are doing. At the same time, we think about our theory and understanding and refine it based on what we have learned from our actions. Through praxis, leaders in organizations can apply their knowledge to create change and utilize their experiences to expand their knowledge.

A major component in democratizing workplace centers around the education of managers and everyone in the workforce. The focus on "reflective thinking" in the adult education field offers a vital tool for the proper design for educating managers to become empowering leaders. The concept of "endullment" and the action research cycle that are both components of the emancipatory branch of adult education are likewise necessary for creating change in the workplace.

This book is for people who work in organizations and who are seeking to enhance their understanding of how to reshape their organization into a more consentaneous setting for productive work.

The adult education tradition contradicts the theorists and practitioners who claim that empowering organizations can only be created when those at the top of the hierarchy decide to share power. The emancipatory education process is the tool of those who work from within systems whether the issue is literacy in a society that controls who can read, civil rights in a society that discriminates, or democracy within an autocratic work system.

From its inception, the adult education movement has linked its purpose with the planting, cultivation, and growth of democratic processes. Early adult education practitioners were closely attuned to the creation of democracy in the workplace. Today, the lessons that have been learned from almost a century of theory and practice are being applied anew to the transformation of the workplace.

1

Some Practical Advice About Empowerment and Democracy

A democracy is more than a form of government; it is primarily a mode of associated living, of conjoint communicated experience.

—John Dewey; *Democracy and Education*

There are two issues that need to be addressed up front in this book for it to serve you as a practical guide to creating an empowering workplace. First, what is meant by the concept of empowerment and workplace democracy? Second, why has the issue of empowerment become important in the contemporary workplace and what does this mean for greater democracy in the workplace?

ON EMPOWERMENT AND DEMOCRACY

There is a reason why many organizational change efforts appear to be short-lived and faddish in their nature. The reason lies in the mental perceptions of the people who attempt to lead or serve as change agents in organizations. The roots of this problem grow from the manner in which people perceive organizations, and themselves as leaders or change agents.

It can be argued that there are two types of mental reference points among those who serve as leaders in organizations. There are those who think from an organic, evolutionary perspective, and who will view even the most radical change as part of the evolutionary process, and there are those who think from a mechanistic point of view, imagining organizations as machines that are built and reassembled, and who search for the right mechanical factors and conditions to achieve success. Put another way, there are those who see their organizations as gardens, and those who see organizations as machines.

Years ago, Myles Horton, at the Highlander Center for Research and Education, made a film that reviewed Highlander's work. In the film, Myles is seen working in his garden, preparing the soil, removing weeds, watering the plants, and finally, harvesting the crop. In between the garden scenes, the viewers watch the story of the civil rights movement, the literacy and citizens' schools, and the struggle to oppose strip mining in Appalachia. Everyone who seeks to create change from within a system should start by thinking like a gardener.

This book is written from the perspective that organizations are organic in their nature and that change based on mechanical models and mechanical thinking is going to fail. The organization can grow and blossom, or wilt and decay, just like roses in a garden. Organizations obey the laws of organic systems much more than the laws of mechanical physics. What organizations and gardens both need are people who are willing to provide vision and planning, and who are willing to get their hands dirty with planting, tending, and weeding, and to harvest the benefits of their efforts. What both need is gardeners.

It is important to begin with this gardening metaphor to properly cultivate an empowering workplace. Organizations are not mechanical clockwork systems. Empowerment is an organic process that must be cultivated and nurtured to thrive.

Figure 1.1
Organizational Models: Organic vs. Mechanical

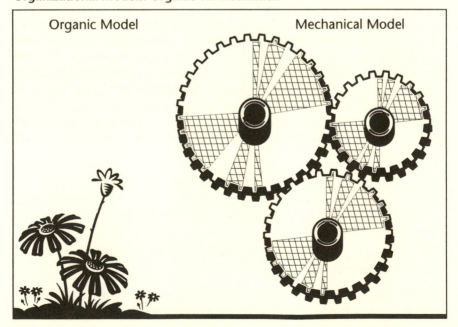

We can not force empowerment on people, and neither can we plan democracy for others. We can only prepare the soil and plant the seeds and hope for growth. Where there is growth, we can nurture and tend the basic experience of empowerment. When an organization becomes an empowering system, we can participate and take pride in what has been created. We can only grow empowering organizations so we must start by thinking of ourselves as organizational gardeners.

WHAT IS EMPOWERMENT?

Empowerment is not a thing. The people I have worked with in creating empowering organizations will state that empowerment is a state of being. In this state of being, people know the boundaries within which they are free to work, and the boundaries are appropriate to their experience and maturity. In an empowering setting, people are engaged in making the decisions that influence the quality of their work life and the quality of the product or service they give their customers. Empowered people have the necessary feedback, training, and knowledge to successfully perform their work. In a state of empowerment, people feel a sense of ownership and pride in their work, and are rewarded for the successful role they play in making their overall organization successful.

No one can order people in the workplace to be empowered. The best you can do is to create a system that reinforces the state of empowerment. Empowerment is not achieved by pep talks or interpersonal relations gimmicks. Either the system in which people work fosters empowerment, or it fosters endullment.

The opposite of empowerment in today's workplace is not oppression. Most of today's workforce is not oppressed. Instead, they are endulled. Endullment is a concept advanced by the educator, Ira Shor, to describe the conditions being observed in school classrooms when the educational system does not allow students to participate in the real learning process. Students turn off the teacher, just as employees turn off the workplace. Students learn how to do the minimum to get by, just as people at work learn how to do the minimum to get by, as their way of staying even with a system they resent.

Empowerment	Endullment
People are involved in making decisions.	People are told what to do.
People have boundaries that are appropriate.	Boundaries are too confining.
People track their own performance.	Feedback only comes from an authority figure, if at all.

| People have a sense of ownership of their work. | People's ownership is very limited. |
| People are proud of their work and their organization. | People are apathetic about their work and their organization. |

To a large extent, the term empowerment has been coopted and is now of very little use. The term is tossed about in the workplace and treated as another management concept. Managers are taught to believe that they can walk around and "zapp" people and make them empowered. Can people be "empowered" when they work in an organization, but do not own the organization itself? Yes, employees in investor-owned companies can certainly be empowered and the decision-making process can be democratic.

Can people working in government-owned enterprises such as those performing road repair, water works, or operating a library be empowered? Of course, if they work for it.

Empowerment and employee ownership are not the same thing. Employee ownership would certainly make it easier to create an empowering and democratic environment. However, empowerment and democracy can flourish in investor-owned and government-owned organizations, just as it is possible for employee-owned companies to be run by autocrats.

WHAT IS WORKPLACE DEMOCRACY?

Workplace democracy is the fruit of the empowerment tree. When the people in an organization are empowered, and the support systems maintain the state of empowerment, then workplace democracy gradually emerges.

Unlike democracy in local government, workplace democracy is not a system of majority rule. Instead, it is a system of consensus decision making. In workplace democracy, people have given their consent to participate and abide by the decisions that are made. In this sense, a workplace democracy is a consentaneous organization, not a majority rule organization.

WHY EMPOWERMENT NOW?

Contemporary interest in workplace empowerment comes from eight forces that are converging in the workplace. These forces are the quality movement, the organizational development discipline, changes occurring in the educational system, the successful experience of employee-owned companies and co-ops, the downsizing of many organizations, the increased level of education of people in the workplace, the growing use of computers that open up communication channels within organizations, and the continued influence of the adult education movement. When the combined forces of these separate factors merge, people start talking about the need for empowering processes in their work place. Let's briefly examine each of these eight forces.

The Quality Movement

The quality movement has introduced many new concepts into the contemporary work place. Dr. W. Edwards Deming has had a major influence in advancing the concept of using statistical tools and in changing our assumptions about how organizations should be led. Dr. Joseph Juran has introduced the concept of involving people in teams to diagnose and fix the quality problems in their work place. Juran's work led eventually to the introduction of quality circles and the wide use of cross-functional teams to solve problems.

Both the quality circle effort and the use of cross-funtional teams have been influencing the manner in which people think about their place of work. Quality circles gave many employees their first taste of participation in decision making at work, but they were short-lived because they were usually a false empowerment, similar to student government in high schools. Cross-functional teams provided many new opportunities for people to participate in decision making in their organizations. Both of these processes have raised the awareness of workers that they are capable of assessing and improving the manner in which work is performed in their organizations.

Managers, likewise, have seen firsthand evidence that the people working with them are capable of assuming greater responsibility. For some managers, it has been an unsettling thought. Others have learned from their experience and have become champions of empowerment within their organizations. No one knows how many supervisors, middle managers, and senior managers are actively working as "empowerment champions" in their organizations. However, they are out there, all across the land. I know them in my own organization, and I have met them from every type of business and in every part of the country.

The Organizational Development Discipline

The organizational development (OD) discipline really began in the 1940s as an academic forum to facilitate the introduction of democracy into the workplace. Every major early practitioner of OD, and the major centers for OD study (such as the National Training Laboratory) started from the point of view of wanting to support empowering processes in the workplace. However, the discipline backed away from that goal during the McCarthy era, and became more academically oriented, and less controversial, over time.

The OD movement today appears to be divided between those who are interested in conducting research to secure their own academic careers, and those who are interested in conducting research and consultation in order to continue the original democratizing purpose of the discipline.

People from the OD perspective have been having some very significant impact in building the conceptual base for creating empowerment. The decades of study of sociotechnical systems redesign, decision-making processes, and communication processes, have created the theoretical base to validate the benefits of consentaneous work systems. The academic community has prepared a small legion of practitioners who are nudging their organizations and clients toward a more significant practice of empowerment. Unfortunately, much of the OD research is written only for consumption by other researchers, more focused on securing academic positions than making a useful contribution to change in the workplace. The great field research methods advanced by William Foote Whyte appear to be ignored in favor of research that wallows in statistics, taking data from the workplace and giving little in return.

Changes in the Educational System

Many adults are being introduced to more empowered decision making through their children's schools. Educational systems all across the country are undergoing a major evolutionary change to create greater local involvement in decision making. Parents are being asked to take a greater role in the governance of their local schools, along with greater empowerment of teachers and local administrators.

The theories and practices of creating more participative schools closely parallel the effort to create empowered workplaces. The principles of empowering education being advanced by educators such as Ira Shor are the mirror image of the principles of empowerment in offices and factories. Indeed, the new perceptions about the adverse impact of authoritarian instruction sheds new light on the problems engendered by autocratic management in the workplace.

In addition to changes in the school systems, there is a growing base of knowledge among adult educators regarding the relationship between democratic practices and the skills and perspectives of adults. A new field, known as reflective practice, has emerged and has started to influence the design of management training and workforce education in ways that will support empowerment. Some of the major contributors in the quality movement, such as Peter Scholtes, have been adult educators, who are applying their discipline to the workplace.

Success of Employee Owned Companies

People are becoming more aware that there are many successful companies today that are owned by their employees. These companies are using their employee-owned status as a marketing tool. During Super-Bowl playoffs, and throughout the year, the public is being asked to accept the principle that employees who own their company are going to be more dedicated to their customers than those who are simply hired hands. Although it may take some time to determine whether or not the public accepts this premise, there is no doubt that the public is being put in a position where it is being asked to accept this proposition.

Most people can accept the notion that people take more care of the automobile they own than the automobile they have rented. No one washes and waxes a rental car. It is not hard to use that analogy to help people understand why employee ownership that shares the benefits of economic success with the workforce could provide a more committed and effective organization.

Downsizing

There can be no doubt that big companies are downsizing. In his most recent book, *Global Paradox,* John Naisbitt noted the strong trend for large companies to want to act and think like small companies. Naisbitt observed the growing concept of "subsidiarity," which he defines as meaning that "power should belong to the lowest possible point in the organization" (p. 8).

This trend for large organizations to want to act like small organizations becomes even more interesting when Naisbitt observes that in both the United States and Germany, over half of the exported products are generated by companies with only nineteen or less employees.

It is not hard to observe that the small organization has not only the advantage of the entrepreneurial spirit, but is much more likely to exhibit highly participative processes in their form of governance. Big organizations clearly tend to place an emphasis on administrative control and tend to bog down in autocracy, unless there is very careful design of the organization. Small organizations can certainly be autocratic, but in many cases, successful entrepreneurs will build their organization by involving their people in the creative and decision-making process.

Increased Levels of Education

In general, the average level of knowledge of today's workforce far surpasses the workforces of any previous era. Today's workers have more formal education and an unbelievable access to information through the electronic media.

The mechanical, and largely autocratic, design of the industrial workplace arose at a time when the average education of the work force was nowhere near the current level of knowledge. Hiearchies and close supervision were necessary when large parts of the workforce were recently arrived from farms or from foreign shores (meaning they were not all fluent in the same language), which posed some problems.

The increased level of education negates many of the reasons why organizations originally created supervisory and managerial positions. This trend will become even more important as today's school students, educated in a more empowering academic climate, enter the workforce in the coming years.

At the same time, the more educated workforce does not value the traditional conflict-based approach of representation advanced by the trade unions. Knowledge workers want to be part of the organization in collaboration and involved. They do not want to be separate and identified with a union that is in conflict with their organization. Knowledge workers want to consent to participate in and be accepted by the organization's leadership for having important ideas and opinions.

Computer Technology

Anyone who has worked in an environment where large numbers of employees have access to computer mail knows that this access to information creates many new patterns of communication. Information used to be passed verbally down through the organization, meeting by meeting. Now, information can be at everyone's desk in a matter of moments. People in different parts of the country are able to share information immediately and make quick decisions by e-mail that used to require travel and meetings.

The enhanced communication systems in the workplace resembles the profusion of printing presses in the colonies that helped foster the drive for democracy among the British colonies. In previous decades, information moved slowly, reinforcing the need for hiearchies and people to help communicate. New computer technology assists organizations in their drive to flatten the organization and act like small business units, thereby providing a rich soil for empowered decision making.

Adult Education

The adult education movement has reached into the workplace through thousands of trainers and educators who are conducting team building, quality improvement, communications training and facilitation. These people enable groups to effectively function and usually have a strong commitment to moving their organization toward greater employee participation.

The emancipatory education branch of adult education has provided a theoretical basis and practical examples for educators to work as field researchers and change agents in human rights, literacy, environmental protection, and other fields. This knowledge is ripe for application in the workplace.

Training and lifelong education has achieved a higher value among today's managers than at any previous time in our history. The heightened awareness of the need for lifelong learning opens the organization for change and the growth of empowering and democratizing processes.

MOVING ON

As with any evolutionary change, it is difficult to predict what the future will become. However, the trends mentioned above appear to reinforce one another, building a synergy that is setting the stage for further change in the culture of the contemporary workplace. With these thoughts in mind, let us now further explore this idea of empowerment in the work place and examine how it can be nurtured in organizations.

APPENDIX:
Opportunities for Praxis

1. How does an organic model help to describe the manner in which your organization functions?

2. Where has the quality movement brought your organization in terms of people wanting higher levels of participation?

3. What type of organizational development efforts have you experienced that help set the stage for fostering empowerment in your organization?

4. What changes are occurring in your community's educational system that are impacting how people around you think about decision making?

5. What employee-owned companies are you aware of? How much ownership do you have in your organization?

6. Has downsizing impacted your organization and the manner in which people want to be involved in decision making?

7. Do people in your organization use e-mail? How does that change the flow of information and the access that people have to what is going on in their organization?

2

Changing the System

When we set the problem, we select what we will treat as the "things" of the situation, we set the boundaries of our attention to it, and we impose upon it a coherence which allows us to say what is wrong and in what directions the situation needs to be changed.

—Donald Schon, *The Reflective Practitioner*

It should be recognized early on that no one can really plan an empowering workplace for other people. People must be involved in the planning process itself for an empowerment effort to be successful. However, there are certain things a change agent will need to know to help people with their planning process. First, it is essential to have a fundamental grasp of the theory of how systems operate to be able to understand what is going to happen when one starts tinkering with a work system. It is the lack of an understanding of systems theory that will cause most empowerment efforts to fail. Second, it helps to have an understanding of how to create change with the under- standing of systems theory. After all, if people are going to change the system, it helps for them to know what the ground rules for change really are. Third, it will be most useful to consider how to apply this systems theory to the cultivation of an empowering workplace.

SYSTEMS THINKING

To work as a gardener and create democratic processes, one must first think about the organization as a living entity that can grow or die. This really requires systems thinking—the understanding of how systems function.

A system is any set of interacting units that have some relationships among them. These component parts are often called subsystems. Each subsystem is constrained by, or dependent on, the other parts of the system. On a microscopic scale, an amoeba is a system. It has smaller subsystems, which must function together for the health of the overall system. On a larger scale, the human body is a system. It has smaller subsystems, such as the respiratory system and the immune system. If any of these subsystems does not function, the health of the larger system is at risk. On an even larger scale, a company (or any other large entity, such as a university, a city government, or a hospital) is a system with subsystems that must all function well for the overall system to be healthy. The nature of a system can be illustrated in Figure 2.1.

A system has an outside boundary that defines its limits. The skin on your body defines the boundary for your physical system. Your subsystems also have boundaries. The veins define the boundaries of the circulatory system. The nerve endings define the boundaries of the nervous system.

Systems vary in the amount of information or material that can come through their boundaries. A closed system allows little outside material or information to enter the system. An open system allows information or material to freely pass through the boundaries. The body's circulatory system is an open system that freely allows oxygen to flow into it from the lungs and out into the body's cells. The body's skin acts as a closed system to keep outside materials from entering the system.

It is important to remember that the subsystems in a system covary,

Figure 2.1
The Elements of a System

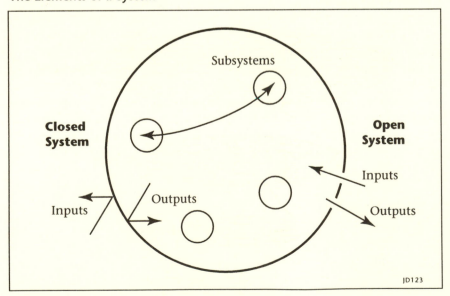

meaning that they impact one another, often in surprising and unpredictable ways. An increase in the work of your respiratory system can cause your skin to change color. A surprising remark can have the same effect.

A Hierarchy of Systems

All systems are part of a hierarchy. You as an individual are a system. Your family is a system, too. It has subsystems, which are the individual family members. Family therapists know that the subsystems covary, meaning that they impact each other in surprising ways. When a child has trouble in school, it is often the result of problems in the family system, such as dysfunctional behavior of a parent that emerges through the child's actions. When treating behavioral problems of a family member, it is often beneficial to bring the whole family system together for discussion and therapy. The subsystem cannot be healed if other parts of the system reopen wounds or continue to create stress.

Work groups are systems, too. The group is made up of individuals who are each a subsystem, and these individuals covary, meaning that they impact each other in many ways. When one member of a group displays dysfunctional behavior, such as coming to work late, it creates many unpredictable responses from the rest of the group.

As in families, therapy for a group system is best handled in a group setting where interactions can be observed and discussed. However, this is rarely done in organizations because we do not like to openly discuss

Figure 2.2
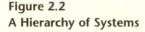
A Hierarchy of Systems

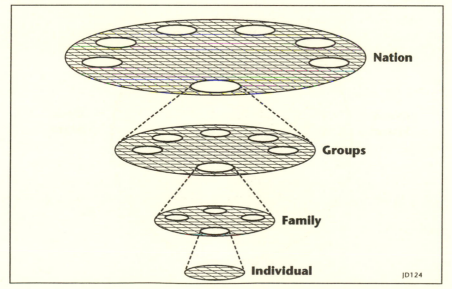

Nation

Groups

Family

Individual

JD124

our problems. We prefer to counsel people in private, which creates another set of unpredictable responses.

A company is a system and has subsystems such as manufacturing, procurement, sales, finance, quality, personnel, and maintenance. Each subsystem of the company will ideally be making decisions and functioning for the good of the whole system. Often, a subsystem loses sight of the overall picture and begins working primarily for its own benefit. Most people in the workplace have firsthand experience with suboptimization which occurs when one part of the company puts its interests above the interests of the entire organization.

A city is a system and has subsystems such as public works, law enforcement, fire protection, revenue collection, and utilities, along with its own unique form or elected leadership. Like the business system, the city subsystems will hopefully be making decisions and functioning for the overall good. The creation of change must take into accout the various subsystems and how they will respond.

An educational system, whether a single college or an entire public school program, is a system and has many subsystems. Again, it is possible for these subsystems to make decisions that will optimize their own interests or the interests of the entire system.

Many methods of reward encourage suboptimization of subsystems. Managers are often measured solely on the performance of their subsystem and not on how well it cooperated with other subsystems. This, of course, has many un- anticipated results which create dysfunction throughout the organization. It does not take much consulting experience to reach the conclusion that most organizational systems have a considerable degree of dysfunctional behavior going on. However, many consultants focus on how to fix one subsystem, which is obviously "broken" or in need of redesign. Few consultants take a systems view of the organization when planning to return the organization to health, and those who try to take a systems perspective are often prohibited from doing so.

Homeostasis

One of the basic rules of systems is that they strive to maintain a balance. This balance, called homeostasis (meaning a dynamic equilibrium), is maintained around some comfortable middle ground. This middle ground, or central tendency, could be a healthy balance of the needs of the subsystems, which leads to a healthy organization. On the other hand, the central tendency could be around an unbalanced trend where one subsystem dominates the rest of the system, causing the total system to become unhealthy.

It does not matter whether the central tendency is a healthy or unhealthy one. It just is. By virtue of what it is, it will also resist change.

Forces for change will be met by counterforces for stability. This is the basic principle of dynamic equilibrium, in which a force for change meets an internal resistance to keep change from occurring.

Of course, Hegel observed this in creating his concept of thesis, antithesis, and synthesis, postulating that out of the exchange of force and counterforce would emerge a new synthesis, and in a sense, this is always true. However, the synthesis you get may not be the synthesis you want. For instance, an organization's push to reduce costs may be countered by employees taking actions that drive away customers or offend the citizens it serves.

Linear vs. Systems Thinking

Those people who do not think in terms of synthesis have an amazingly simple belief that change occurs in a linear cause and effect manner. To create change you do A, which leads to B, and then leads to C, as shown in Fugure 2.3. To create employee involvement one only needs to define a process, train the people, and then they will go out and implement what they have been trained to do. When the linear process fails to achieve our expectations we blame the people involved. They must not have been good trainers. They were not aggressive enough in pushing an idea. They were lazy. We don't stop to consider that our thinking process is completely out of touch with the reality of the systems in which we exist.

Change in a system involves feedback. Someone does A, which starts

Figure 2.3
Linear Change and Change in Systems

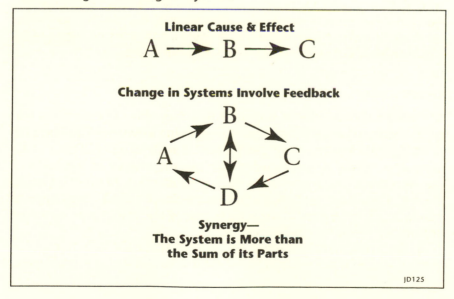

to lead to B, but B talks to D and they decide to go see C who has a different slant on things, so then D goes to A to propose something different. Where did things go wrong? They didn't. This is normal. In any organization there are many people who believe they are in control. In a sense they are right, because they probably have a greater degree of power than other people in the organization. But everyone in the organization has power, from the the Chief Executive Officer to the janitor. Everyone influences other parts of the system, therefore, no one is ever really in control of a system. It has a life of its own due to the countless interactions that go on every day.

Systems create synergy, meaning that the whole is more than the sum of its parts. Synergy is the result of all the countless interactions that release energy in the organization. All organizations have synergy. Some synergy spins the organization in an upward spiral of success. Other synergy spins the organization in a downward spiral of defeat. Synergy is there in any system whether you like it or not. The challenge is to create an upward spiral of positive energy instead of allowing a downward spiral to occur. Watch what happens in a football game when one team starts to pull ahead. They pick up enthusiasm and start to do even better. The team being left behind often seems to lose energy and do even worse. These are both examples of synergy. It is a rare team in any setting that can reverse this phenomenon. It usually requires the skill of an expert organizational gardener, or leader who can hold people steady in the face of defeat and create a comeback.

So, rather than looking at your organization as a pyramid, or an upside down pyramid (a harmless and useless notion), or as a circle with concentric layers, start thinking of your organization as a seething, breathing, mass of wriggling globs that have thousands of interactions on a daily basis that no one can begin to predict. Try thinking of management as the central nervous system. Perhaps production is the heart and sales the lungs of your system. Just keep in mind that all of the subsystems covary, meaning that they impact each other in very surprising ways.

CHANGING A SYSTEM

The organizational gardener's role is to help the system change from within so that it encourages the creation of empowering processes. Since we are now thinking in terms of systems, we need to ask, how do systems change?

One must start with the understanding that systems do not want change. By their nature they seek a consistent, stable, central tendency. However, to survive, systems often need change in order to achieve a state of health. The gardener's job is to introduce change into the system, knowing full well that the system is going to resist and react in unpredictable ways. To maintain their comfortable balance, systems create rules. There are two types of rules to struggle within the system, the written rules (formalized as policies and procedures) and the unwritten rules (informal behavioral expectations).

Written rules are created to protect the interests of a particular subsystem, and sometimes to protect the overall health of the total system. The Human Resources organization establishes rules to govern hiring, discipline, and other processes to protect the organization from law suit and provide an orderly flow of work. The rules also protect the Human Resources subsystem. Quality establishes rules to protect the organization from shipping a substandard product. The same rules also reinforce the role and position of the Quality subsystem within the total system.

STAGES OF CHANGE

There are many ways to describe how change occurs and the pace at which it can occur in the organization. Let's look at how change occurs and then at the different paces at which it may occur, as shown in Figure 2.4.

There are three stages in change in a system. The first stage involves softening up the change target and getting it ready. This has been called unfreezing the current system. It's often called an education phase. Some call this early encounter, awareness of impending change, and developing a positive perception of the coming change. It means rototilling the ground and spreading the manure. Any way you want it, the change has to be broadcast to people in the system. Here it comes! This is what it means! Here's how you can help or get mangled!

The second stage of change is the implementation phase. This means making the change, installing it, doing it, cutting out the old and inserting the new, putting the plant in the soil. Stop talking about it and do it!

The third stage of change is to make things normal again, refreeze the system, reinforce new behaviors, institutionalize and internalize. It's the new world order. It's the way it is, so get used to it. The fight's over, let's get on with doing some work around here. It's new growth, so learn to deal with it.

The proper pace for change depends on many factors. How major a change is this? How much cooperation do you need? How much shock can the system tolerate? How urgent is the need to change? How strong are the forces for change?

Some approaches to empowerment can be slow paced, with low shock from change. There's plenty of time to get people used to the idea. People can gradually try out various methods and experiement with new skills and decision-making processes. Slow-paced change also gives the forces of opposition the maximum opportunity to resist, but allows them to eventually become a part of the new synthesis.

Rapid-paced change is better when the shock of change will be great to the organization. Let's not take all week to perform surgery. Let's get on with it so we can start healing. The major difference between gradual empowerment and a more focused change process, such as sociotechnical systems redesign, is the pace of change and the amount of shock the change will present to the system.

Systems can die from shock. Plants die from the shock of being moved. People die from the shock of losing a part of the family system. Organizations die from the shock of a merger or the trauma of a layoff, so before you plan your change, think about how much shock is involved. What pace is in the best interest of your system? Also, think about the strength of the system to endure shock. Surgery is great on a healthy young person whose subsystems are all in good shape, but fatal for an older person with weak subsystems. If you are going to move a plant, think about the readiness of the soil to receive the plant. Reengineering can be a great way to produce shocking change in a short time frame if the soil is ready for the new arrival. A reengineered process will fail if the soil is not well prepared.

Force Field Analysis

Kurt Lewin, the German social scientist, created an image of change as involving a force field, as illustrated in Figure 2.5. The amount that a sys-

Figure 2.4
Stages of Change

Unfreezing	Contact Clearly Encountered Awareness of Change Understanding Change Positive Perception	Education
Change	Installation Adoption	Do
Refreeze	Institutionalization Internalize	Reinforce

JD126

tem will change is determined by the forces that will support and resist the change. Change involves the balance of driving forces and restraining forces. One can create change by strengthening the driving forces and weakening the restraining forces. The greatest benefit might come from energy spent on weakening restraining forces, thus removing the oppositions strength, or will to resist.

Lewin's concept can be applied in a multitude of settings that involve changing systems. On the individual level, behavioral change occurs when the forces supporting change have more influence than the forces that resist the change. Individuals may have a strong desire to stop smoking, but the force that resists the change can be stronger than the forces that encourage the change.

In a family setting, there may be a desire to spend more time together in conversation. The driving force may be the need to communicate and get to know one another. The resisting force may be the desire to watch the news on television. The family's behavior will be determined by which of these two forces is stronger.

In a work setting, there are multiple forces at play around any issue, especially the question of empowerment. Before launching into an effort to create an empowering workplace, the effective organizational gardener will apply the force field methodology to the specific workplace to determine the forces that will support empowerment and the forces that will discourage it.

For instance, in seeking to introduce a more participative leadership style

Figure 2.5
Kurt Lewin's Force Field Analysis

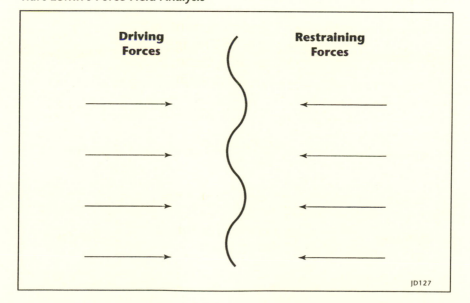

in an organization, people may develop a force field analysis to assess the situation and to develop a strategy for change. An analysis may result in a chart like this.

Forces Opposed To Greater Participation	Forces Supporting Greater Participation
Current supervisors feel threatened.	Need for more flexibility to meet customer needs.
Some employees will refuse to be more participative.	Need to reduce costs by having fewer managers.
Some supervisors lack the skills to be participative leaders.	Educated employees expect to participate.
Employees may have new ideas management does not like.	Need to identify more ideas for improving work systems.

In preparing a plan based on this analysis, the gardener may seek to weaken the opposing forces by educating supervisors and employees about the benefits and methods for participation. However, since the change will occur within a system, it should be recognized that more education to weaken resistance will also strengthen the force related to employee's expectations to participate. Change will not be a linear process and the consequences of introducing change should be fully explored.

Consequences of Change

Joseph Juran was closer to a systems view when he observed that change in an organization always involves two areas, the technical change and the social consequences of the change. Reading an article by Margaret Mead on South Sea cultures, Juran saw the workplace as a culture with distinct norms and values. Change threatens to upset the norms, so, as in all systems, change is resisted.

Systems resist change, according to Juran's model, by resisting the technical change, while the real resistance may be the unspoken fear of the social consequences of the change. Juran noted that railway workers resisted the diesel locomotive, stating that it was unsafe to have an engineer alone in the engine. They really feared the loss of the jobs of the firemen (a social consequence).

Juran's observation is an important part of understanding the unpredictable manner in which change occurs within a system. People resist a change, but offer a reason for their resistance that is often different from their real reason. How do you cope with that in your linear A leads to B leads to C mind set?

Oddly enough, this is where Lewin's idea of weakening the resisting forces is best applied. When the change agent is in the first phase of change (unfreezing, educating, rototilling, and developing a positive perception), this is the time to identify what social consequences will be forthcoming and find ways to minimize negative results, which will create resistance.

Juran suggested that change occurs when innovators are able to show the mass of people in a system how a change will benefit them. Few people, according to Juran, volunteer for change, but they will gladly change when they start to see others benefiting from the change.

Juran also suggested that a small number of inhibitors will resist change because it threatens their status or influence in the system. The resistance will come in the form of plausible reasons why the new idea will not work. Rarely does the resister admit the deeper social reasons for fighting the change.

Summarizing Systems and Change

Your organization is a system. It does not react to change in a linear, predictable, manner. Therefore you have to develop a plan that creates multiple points of intervention to create a sustained migration toward democracy.

To create a sustained movement toward democracy in your organization, you must plan strategies that address all three phases of change, the educational phase, the implementation phase, and the reinforcing phase.

Healthy change fails when people are not equipped educationally to know what to do, when to do it, and how to do it. Keeping the poor illiterate keeps them from gaining power. Keeping the employees from understanding the budget keeps them from participating in the decision-making process.

Healthy change fails when people are educated but not empowered to implement what they have learned. You may teach someone to read, but then deny them access to the library. You may teach employees how to diagnose quality problems, but then deny them time to apply their knowledge. In this phase, people need to know that the time for change has begun, it's okay for me to change, and in fact, it's a part of my job.

Healthy change fails when the new behaviors are not reinforced and treated as normal. You may encourage everyone to work together as a team, but then watch teamwork fall apart when you reward them individually for their contributions.

Change intervention must have components directed at all parts of the system. From the inside of the management system to those on the boundaries who have contact with customers and suppliers, and in every staff,

lab, production, or maintenance subsystem, there must be a plan for intervention.

APPLYING SYSTEMS THEORY TO THE CREATION OF
EMPOWERING SYSTEMS IN THE WORKPLACE

The creation of an empowering workplace requires a change strategy
that will harness all the known attributes of systems theory. The strategy
will require an understanding of the organization's boundaries, the counterforces that will seek to retain homeostasis, a plan to unfreeze the system, the creation of champions to reinforce the movement, and support
systems that will reinforce the concept of democratic participation.

Assessing the Boundaries

Those who are going to create a strategy for fostering empowerment
in an organization need to start by assessing the organization's boundaries
to determine the sources of external information that will be helpful in
creating the setting for change.

Who are the outside people or organizations that people inside your
organization listen to? Is there a particular company or group that your
organization accepts as a model or a group to be emulated? How willing
will people in your organization be to get involved in benchmarking? How
strong is the "not invented here" syndrome in your organization?

If your organization has open boundaries, then the planners can bring
in external information to help set the stage for greater participation.
Companies that practice greater participation can be benchmarked by people from your organization. Books and magazine articles will be helpful
in advancing the proposition.

If your organization has closed boundaries or a strong tendancy to deval-
ue any ideas "not invented here," then the strategy must focus on invent-
ing it here. The role of internal champions becomes much more important.

Anticipate the Resistance

Knowing that systems automatically create resistance to change, it only
makes sense to anticiapte that resistance early on and make plans to deal
with it. Start with a force field analysis to identify who will support and
who will oppose greater participation. Then make plans to strenthen the
supporters and address the concerns of the opponents.

It is vital to work from the point of view that those people who favor
autocratic control of the workplace do so out of genuine concern for the
organization, and not simply out of a selfish desire to maintain power. If

you dismiss people's resistance to change as due only to personal aggrandizement, you will lose all hope of being able to effectively persuade them to support your effort. The chapter on creating team leaders will offer some specific ideas regarding how to address the concerns of those who have concerns about becoming more democratic in their leadership.

Preparing to the Pathway to Empowerment

There are seven basic steps along the pathway to empowerment that must be addressed in the change process. The exact sequence of these steps may differ from one organization to another, depending on what actions have already taken place. However, in general, these seven steps will need to be covered to begin to create an empowering organization.

First, there needs to be a group of empowerment champions in the organization's leadership that will support the overall empowerment process. The makeup of the empowerment champions will naturally differ from one organization to another, but without these champions, the empowerment effort has little hope of being accepted by the organization.

Second, the empowerment champions need to create a legitimate team or pannel that will represent the interests of all the various people in the organization. This group should serve as an empowerment planning team. The actual name of the team or committee will vary with every organization, but in most cases, some type of reperesentative team needs to exist that can allow all the people in the organization to participate in the movement toward empowerment.

Third, there must be an organized process to help the existing leadership change its leadership style toward a participative approach that fosters empowerment. This means training that addresses both cognitive thinking processes and interpersonal skills.

Fourth, there must be education for the people in the workforce that offers them the knowledge and tools they need to be able to effectively expand their boundaries and work together to achieve their organizational mission.

Fifth, the basic support systems of the organization, such as compensation, appraisal, performance indicators, employment, and others, need to be realigned to support empowerment instead of fostering endullment.

Sixth, there must be team meetings where people can use consensus decision making. There must also be a consensus regarding the types of issues that should not be decided by consensus.

Seventh, the people in the organization need to be brought into the strategic and tactical planning process of the organization so that they can have a sense of ownership.

Seven Step Path To Empowerment
1. Create champions.
2. Involve people in planning the change.
3. Create team leaders.
4. Educate the workforce.
5. Change the support systems.
6. Practice consensus decision making.
7. Involve people in strategic and tactical planning.

When these steps are addressed, the basic needs of the entire system are being met. An effort to create empowerment that does not address all of these areas will be perceived as a failure, either by the leadership or the people within the organization.

FINDING THE EMPOWERMENT CHAMPIONS

Empowerment champions are managers and supervisors who have personally adopted an empowering style of leadership. This adoption may be consistant with the values and behaviors of their superiors and peers, or it might be quite an exception to those around them.

The mark of an empowerment champion is in their actions, not their words. There are many people who talk about empowering the people in their organization. There are many who want the organization to be more empowering, but whose personal behavior endulls the people who work in their part of the organization.

The true champion of empowerment has demonstrated his or her dedication to this concept by pioneering some innovative ideas in the part of the organization under their influence. This person may have pioneered an empowered work team, or may have championed a cross-functional team that gave employees unusual lattitude and involvement in decision making.

Often, the empowerment champion is a line manager who has learned from personal experience that people perform better when they are encouraged to make decisions and have a sense of ownership over the work they are doing. Some people become empowerment champions because of an appeal to theory, but most are champions due to their own experiences and observations of what really works.

Some empowerment champions are in support staff positions, such as Human Resources or Quality. These managers are often more likely to have reached their perspective on empowerment due to a combination of personal experience and on theory. The staff members of these support groups have a role to play that can be equal in value to that of the line managers who gravitate in this direction.

Role of the Empowerment Champions

The role of the empowerment champions is to champion. This means to serve as advocates and to assess the conditions supporting an empowered state of being within the organization. The champions serve as a caucus group within the organization. Out of loyalty to the organization, and a conviction that empowerment works, these people band together to talk about what needs to be done to change the organization, and then they set the wheels in motion.

The empowerment champions are advocates to their follow managers. They speak on behalf of empowering actions in staff meetings. They point out the successes of empowerment efforts within their own organization and from other organizations. They defend the concept in meetings when others want to continue excessive centralized, top-down control of the organization.

The empowerment champions are advocates to their employees. They lead by example, creating zones of empowerment within their parts of the organization. They encourage their people to experiment with new approaches to management. They support training that will lead to empowering people.

The empowerment champions are advocates to each other, giving one another support when the movement appears weak. They assess where the bottlenecks to empowerment are in the organization, and develop strategies to work around these impediments.

Finally, the empowerment champions are the people who arrange for the organization to create some form of a study team, quality council, empowerment committee, or whatever it may be called, to involve people in the organization in the movement toward empowerment. The champions recognize that empowerment is not something they can do to people, but it is a state of being that they can work with people to create. The champions work their organizational system to give legitimacy to the creation of a group that will include all the viewpoints within the organization. They champion the work of this planning team, give advice on how it should proceed, and listen to proto-presentations from the group.

The change agent (organizational gardener) needs to identify the empowerment champions and encourage them to work together, to share information, and to form a strategy for helping the entire organization pursue the pathway to empowerment.

Obviously the entire empowerment process will be greatly enhanced when the senior manager in an organization is an empowerment champion. That is the ideal situation that everyone should hope to have for their organization. Sometimes, the senior manager is close to being a champion, and with the encouragement and evidence supplied by middle managers, can decide to comfortably lead the empowerment process. Sometimes the senior managers does not have the empowerment issue on his or her screen. In that case, the empowerment champions within the organization will play a vital role in advancing the empowerment concept and providing pockets of success that make empowerment a viable concept in an organization.

APPENDIX:
Opportunities for Praxis

1. What are the major subsystems in your organization and how do they covary?

2. What are examples of change efforts in your organization that have failed? How did these efforts address or fail to address systems issues?

3. Where is your organization in terms of the seven step path to empowerment?

4. Who are the empowerment champions in your organization?

5. Create a force field analysis showing the forces in your organization that support and oppose empowering people.

3

Creating an Empowerment Planning Team and Creating Team Leaders

We stand in need of a revolution of the mind—not a mere exchange of power groups—before an economic revolution can transform industry into a cooperative enterprise, before "power over" is transposed into "power with" in industry.
—Eduard Lindeman, *The Meaning of Adult Education*

In assessing the state of empowerment in their organization, the empowerment champions will find that they cannot take unilateral actions that will foster empowerment. They must involve people in the organization to come up with the best form of empowerment for their particular organizational situation.

There are many issues that the champions will encounter right off the bat that require input from the employees in the organization. What do employees think about the current situation? What do the supervisors think about the current situation? What do the support organizations think? To answer these questions, the champions need to have the organization create a legitimized group that can pursue these and other issues.

The champions will often perceive that a hard drive toward empowerment will be met with a great deal of resistance from within the management ranks and from some employees, as is natural for any system. Employee and management's buy-in to the design of the movement toward empowerment is vital to success. Employee and supervisor's buy-in is essential for people to accept the changes and cooperate to make the change successful.

So, one of the first issues for the empowerment champions is to help the organization create an empowerment planning team.

Seven Step Path to Empowerment
1. Create champions.
➤ *2. Involve people in the planning process.*
3. Create team leaders.
4. Educate the workforce.
5. Change the support systems.
6. Practice consensus decision making.
7. Involve people in strategic and tactical planning.

CREATING AN EMPOWERMENT PLANNING TEAM

An empowerment Planning team is a legitimate grassroots planning team that will involve a diagonal cross section of the people and perspectives in the organization. It is legitimate in that its role to plan for the migration toward an empowering environment has been agreed to and sanctioned by the management of the organization. If the planning team lacks this legitimacy, then its meetings will be filled with self-doubt as to whether or not the team's recommendations will even be heard by the organization.

The team is said to be grassroots because it is designed to hear people's perspectives about what is going on, not just the view of the managers.

Figure 3.1
Membership of an Empowerment Planning Team

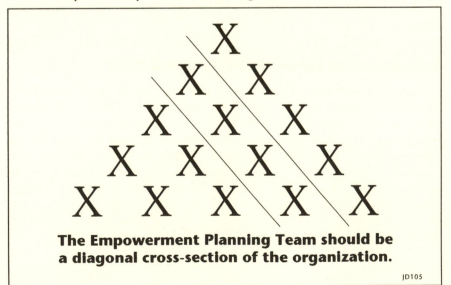

The Empowerment Planning Team should be a diagonal cross-section of the organization.

JD105

Members of this team might be invited by management to participate, but they should not be appointed by management. It will be even more effective if the members of this planning team are selected by their peers to represent their interests and point of view.

By being a diagonal cross section of the organization, the team will have people from middle management, front-line supervision, and all of the various work groups in the organization. For instance, in a city government, the team might include a department manager, a supervisor, a police officer, a fire fighter, a refuse worker, a librarian, or others. In a factory, the team would include a middle manager, one or two front-line supervisors, a secretary, production workers, engineers, and other groups within the facility. In a school, the team would include administrators, faculty, and students. In this manner, all of the organizational units are represented and all the various points of view are assembled together.

CHARTER FOR THE EMPOWERMENT PLANNING TEAM

To be effective, most teams need a charter that defines the boundaries of the team's authority and responsibilities. A charter gives the team a formal statement that it has the right to research and make recommendations regarding changes in the organization that will foster a climate of empowerment. The team might even be granted implementation rights within its boundaries, but in most cases, the team's role is to study and recommend and assess the effectiveness of changes that are agreed to by management.

The empowerment champions need to play a role in defining the charter of the planning team. The champions can assure that the team will be given the broadest possible boundaries within the context of their organization.

THE ROLE OF THE EMPOWERMENT PLANNING TEAM

Planning teams can provide a variety of roles, but there are some common and essential activities that should be included within their charter. First, the team needs to assess the readiness of the organization for making change, identifying barriers to empowerment. Second, the team should identify training needs and participate in getting the training implemented that will "unfreeze" the current state of the organization. The team should be involved in planning how the empowerment effort will be communicated to the workforce. This team will also evaluate the progress being made in the empowerment effort and can help plan changes to the empowerment strategy once it is under way.

Roles of the Empowerment Planning Team
1. Assess the organization's readiness.
2. Identify training needs.
3. Support implementation of training.
4. Plan communication to the workforce.
5. Evaluate the progress of empowerment.

It is not the planning team's role to carry out a senior manager's plan for "empowerment." The planning team is to create the plan, based on its assessment of the organization's current situation. The team's strategy must be based on a pragmatic view of how far and how fast the organization can move, not on an idealistic wish.

ASSESSING THE ORGANIZATION'S READINESS

This step for the empowerment planning team is usually accomplished through the use of a force field analysis. The team members identify the forces that are conducive to empowerment and those forces that lead to endullment. Then the team decides how to strengthen the empowering forces and weaken the endulling forces.

IDENTIFYING TRAINING NEEDS

There are two main issues for the empowerment planning team (EPT) to address regarding training that supports empowerment. First of all, how does an organization take supervisors and managers who have been successful contributors to the organization, based on autocratic leadership practices, and help them develop skills as participative leaders? Second, how does an organization reach out to the workforce and prepare people to participate in an empowered manner? The first question will be the subject of the remainder of this chapter. The second question will be addressed in Chapter 4.

The EPT should consider how the current supervisors in the organization are perceived. Many supervisors see themselves as being fairly participative in their leadership style. They often think that they are much more participative than the supervisors they used to work under in their own earlier years. However, the perceptions of the supervisor's employees may not match the view of the supervisors.

In many cases, the planning team will determine that it will be effective to transition from work groups that are led by a supervisor to teams that are led by a facilitator, or team leader. Often, this is only a matter of changing the current supervisor's leadership style. Sometimes, planning teams opt for moving to self-directed work teams.

The term *self-directed work team* indicates that there is not an immediate supervisor or facilitator assigned to the team. There may be a facilitator that the team shares with other teams, or there will be a manager that the team reports to, but who does not direct the work of the team on a daily basis.

The empowered team with a facilitator is an interim style of empowerment, between the supervisor-led work group and the self directed team. In many organizations, the use of team leaders, or facilitators, provides a smooth transition on the path to empowerment.

CREATING TEAM LEADERS

Supervisors are thought to resist empowerment and to cling to autocratic behaviors because they fear loss of influence, loss of a familiar career path, and they have doubts that an empowered team will really work.

There are several conditions that must be created to help leaders shift from autocratic to democratic behaviors. First, there must be an opportunity for supervisors to reflect on the structure of their organization, their role as a leader, and the data that have been collected over many decades on leadership styles.

Second, there must be a time for building skills which are essential to democratic leadership. People need a safe place to practice using new behavioral skills. They need time to see for themselves that they can achieve more through empowering behaviors.

Third, there must be a specific plan for change which prevents comfortable autocrats from avoiding the reflective thinking and skill building process, which lead to change.

And fourth, there should be a coach to observe and follow up on the

Table 3.1
Comparison of Endulling and Empowering Work Systems

Endulling	Empowering	
Traditional Work Group	**Facilitated Team**	**Self-Directed Team**
Supervisor makes assignments.	Facilitator helps team decide.	Team makes assignments.
Supervisor reviews performance indicators.	Entire team reviews indicators.	Team reviews indicators.
Supervisor leads meetings.	Facilitator leads meetings.	Team leads its own meetings.
Supervisors leads.	Facilitator coaches.	Team leads itself.

change process with each supervisor.

Conditions Necessary for Transition
From Traditional to Empowered Team Leadership
1. Reflection on roles and styles.
2. Skill building.
3. Specific plan to follow.
4. Coaches to assist in the change.

Assessing the Needs

Although this chapter defines a variety of skills that supervisors need to function effectively as participative leaders, no one should automatically assume that all of these skill areas require a new training effort in every organization. One of the first rules of good adult education is to not try to teach people what they already know. The empowerment champions, or the human resources or organizational development staff supporting the empowerment effort, should assess the organization to determine what skills and concepts have already been taught. The focus should then be on closing the gaps between what supervisors already know and the remaining skills needed to give them a complete set of skills.

The problem with much of the supervisory training of the last three decades resides in the absence of a defined set of skills required to foster empowerment. There has been no shortage of supervisory training designed to reinforce autocratic control. There has also been a good deal of training that provided a backdoor approach to empowering leadership, but until recently, very little thought has been given to the systematic definition of the leadership skills necessary to generate empowering work conditions.

Reflecting on Leadership Roles

Most supervisors are aware of problems that occur every day that are warning signs that autocratic leadership works poorly, such as employee alienation, fear of reprisal, and endullment. However, the warnings are filtered out because they do not fit accepted beliefs about how a supervisor should behave. These beliefs, after all, were acquired over time, reinforced, and nurtured.

The process of learning a new leadership role begins by engaging supervisors and managers in thinking reflectively to challenge their established beliefs about what constitutes effective leadership. Reflective thinking can be encouraged by asking supervisors to draw a picture of what their organization looks like. In this nonthreatening exercise, people allow their unfiltered observations to slip out and are often surprised at the pictures they create.

For example, one group of supervisors participating in this activity pictured their employees as a column of ants marching along toward a hill, as illustrated in Figure 3.2. Supervision was seen as a cloud raining on the parade. Another group of supervisors drew a picture of employees running for their lives from a tornado labeled as "upper management." On the other hand, a group of people in an empowered team doing this same exercise drew their team as people in a boat rescuing their customers who were in the water around them.

The point of this activity is to allow the images that people have about their organization to come out in a new way. This gives people an opportunity to reflect on beliefs about their organization, which they may not have been ready to openly discuss.

Role Playing

People often learn a great deal from taking part in role-playing exercises that allow them to experience the problems associated with working under autocratic leadership. Many organizations use role play, which requires supervisors to work together to make some product such as a paper airplane or a frisbee from a paper plate. Productivity under autocratic leadership, which controls information and discourages creativity, is compared with productivity in an empowered setting.

Role playing allows supervisors to discover for themselves the disadvantages associated with autocratic leadership. Self-discovery of the prob-

Figure 3.2
A View of the Organization

**Supervisors pictured their employees as
ants marching through the rain.**

JD106

lems of autocracy provides a much more profound experience than hearing about it in a lecture or videotape.

A Little Dose of Research Data

After supervisors have had a chance to do some self-discovery and reflect on how their behavior restricts the productivity of their organization, it's time for just a bit of theory.

Many people are intrigued to learn that Kurt Lewin proposed a model for democratic leadership in 1945. Lewin observed that there were clear differences between autocratic and democratic leadership. He added the observation that in moving away from an autocratic style, some people tended to drift into a laissez-faire style, which is an abandonment of leadership, not a leadership style. Democratic leadership, according to Lewin, is an active style that fosters participation, not a passive style that forfeits leadership.

Leland Bradford and Ronald Lippitt, who were also writing in 1945, elaborated on Lewin's model by observing that the autocratic style could actually be divided into hard-boiled autocrats and benevolent autocrats. The distinction was that benevolent autocrats temper their controlling behavior through the use of human relations skills.

Robert Tannenbaum and Warren Schmidt followed in this line of thinking in the 1950s by creating a leadership model that offered a continuum of decision making behaviors, ranging from boss-centered to team-centered

Figure 3.3
Research of the 1950s

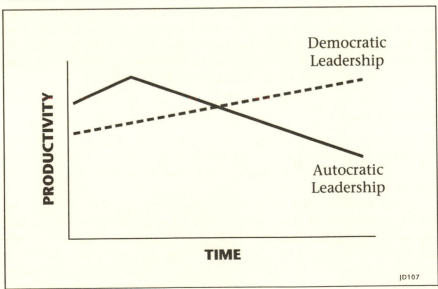

approaches.

Much of the research of the 1950s and 1960s, such as the work of Lester Coch and John French, Stanley Seashore, and Rensis Likert, can be summarized in Figure 3.3.

In a variety of studies that took specific factories and experimented with productivity based on autocratic and participative leadership, it can be seen that autocratic leadership can spark an initial, short-term increase in productivity. People will work harder, at first, when placed under tighter control. However, this control leads to higher turnover (the best people leave), and general employee resistance to the autocratic control in the forms of increased absenteeism and apathy. Over time, the workforce becomes endulled and the productivity falls.

Empowering leadership compares well with the performance of autocratic leadership in the short run, and in the long run builds higher and sustained productivity, lower turnover, lower absenteeism, and greater employee commitment to the organization.

This information, based on several research studies, is greatly reinforced by the data published in 1949 from the War Production Board by Dorothea de Schweinitz, which documented hundreds of cases of tremendous productivity improvements in American industry during the war years when management adopted more participative leadership practices.

All of this research data leads supervisors to an embarrassing question. If we have known about the benefits of empowering leadership and empowered teams for many decades, why have we done so little to implement these ideas?

Part of the answer may be found in the short-term improvement in performance that autocratic leadership offers. When pressed to make changes, and when needing to have a visible impact in the short run, using an autocratic leadership style offers an immediate method for obtaining visible improvement. If the autocratic manager is fortunate, or shrewd, he or she will move on to another assignment before the long-term consequences of endullment are felt throughout the organization.

Provide a Model

Giving supervisors a model for describing the various styles of leadership helps tremendously. The problem is, which model should you use? Why not make up your own that combines several theories tailored to your specific organization or situation?

Figure 3.4 is a model that combines elements of Lewin, Bradford and Lippitt, Tannenbaum and Schmidt, and a few other observations. This model shows a continuum from hard-boiled autocratic behavior to fully participative (or empowering) leadership. Along the continuum will be seen the benevolent autocrat and the consultative leader who asks for input and then makes decisions.

How about the "reluctant autocrat" in this model? That describes the leader who would like to be more empowering but does not think it would be accepted by management or the workers. There is strong reason to believe that the majority of supervisors in today's workplace are in the "reluctant autocrat" role, hopeful for the opportunity to be more participative, but uncertain that participative leadership will be supported by their higher management.

This model can also be used to admonish leaders to watch out for taking the downward slide into letting people run amok by abdicating leadership responsibility and becoming what Kurt Lewin called a laissez-faire leader.

Ready to Learn New Skills

When autocratic leaders have had the opportunity to reflect on their situation and consider some evidence to realign their thinking, they are ripe for acquiring new empowering behaviors. Learning new behaviors requires careful preparation in a somewhat structured learning environment.

The big question is, what behaviors constitute those needed for empowering leadership? A review of several surveys and case studies offers the following skills that supervisors need to master to practice empowering leadership:

Figure 3.4
An Organizational Model

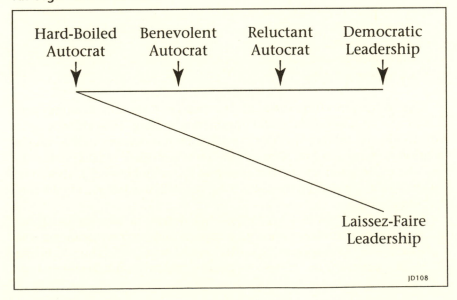

JD108

- the ability to lead participative meetings;
- listening skills;
- the ability to handle conflict;
- the knowledge for establishing measures;
- group centered decision making skills and consensus-building skills;
- teaching skills; and
- teambuilding skills.

Leading Participative Meetings

Empowering leaders need to gather the team together for regular meetings. The meeting is necessary for the team to study data, make decisions, identify problems, make plans, and learn about issues. It is the team leader's responsibility to ensure that an agenda is developed and that the team focuses some time on its performance measures. The team leader tracks issues from the last meeting for follow-up and highlights urgent issues for immediate resolution. The team leader ensures that once a decision is reached, someone accepts responsibility for implementation.

Team leaders make sure that there is a regular time for the meeting and minimize interruptions. The team leader ensures that there are tools, such as flip charts, and works on achieving 100 percent attendance at that meeting. Responsibility for running the meeting might rotate from person to person (an idea advanced in the Harvard Business Review over a decade ago).

To effectively facilitate empowering meetings, a leader needs to be able to help people perform a variety of functions. Key meeting functions are
- Exploration/identification of issues and concerns;
- Planning-both strategic and tactical;
- Decision making;
- Problem solving;
- Status updates; and
- Information sharing.

Empowering meetings cover all six processes. Endulling meetings generally focus on status updates and information sharing. The planning function will be the subject of Chapter 8. Chapter 6 is devoted to the issue of decision making. Chapter 4 covers the skills necessary for problem solving. The exploration and identification of issues and concerns should be covered before moving on to other leadership skills needed outside the context of meetings.

At any point in time, a system or a subsystem, or an individual, has many different concerns, issues, and opportunities to be considered. On a regular basis, the empowering leader should engage the team in listing all of the opportunities, issues, concerns, problems, and deadlines confronting it.

After the list has been developed, the leader should ensure that each issue has been identified in a specific manner so that all team members understand what each item means. Then the leader should ask team members to weed out the issues that may be beyond the group's ability to influence, such as "peace in the Middle East," and set these aside in a "too hard" pile. These are the issues that the group does not have the energy or ability to address at this time. Timing may be bad, or the group may need more clout or allies to take on these issues.

The remaining active issues should be prioritized based on the seriousness of each item, the availability of time and resources to address each item, and the relative urgency that each item presents to the group.

Exploring/Identifying Concerns
- Generate list of issues, concerns, ideas, problems, and deadlines.
- Clarify the issues on the list.
- Screen out the "too hard" pile.
- Prioritize the "active" issues.
- Plan actions to address issues.

After prioritizing the issues list, a plan of attack needs to be developed for the highest priority items. Over time, the empowering leader can pass the process of exploring and identifying issues and opportunities over entirely to the team members.

Learning to Listen

Effective leaders have strong listening skills to understand situations, improve cooperation, and encourage people to take responsibility. "Active listening," as defined by Carl Rogers, causes the listener to try to grasp the facts and the feelings of what is being communicated. The listener reflects both facts and feelings back to the speaker to ensure that correct communication has occurred.

The goal of listening is to be able to respond to the speaker's needs, not our own. We should keep listening even when the speaker's ideas and actions are different from our own. A good listener will respond with empathy, withhold judgment, listen with the eyes, and squint with the ears.

Empowering leaders need an opportunity to practice active listening by working in small groups to practice reflecting the facts and feelings being shared by others. They need to practice responding to peoples' feelings about issues, noting all the cues, and testing for understanding.

There are two effective approaches to teaching listening skills. If supervisors have had little exposure and practice with active listening, then they need an in-class opportunity to learn these skills.

The instructor should first demonstrate the active listening process to the group by providing an example where he or she gives feedback that demonstrates acknowledgment of both the facts and feelings offered by another person. Then, the supervisors should be divided into triads to practice active listening. Each member should have the opportunity to play the role of a listener, a person with a problem, and a critiquer. Each triad should have a set of prompts to initiate the practice conversations, such as

I really don't like the way that I have to work so much more overtime than everyone else in this group.

I'm tired of being the only person who will clean up around the coffee pot.

I think we're letting our telephones go on ringing and ringing and our customers don't like it very much.

Special prompts can be developed for specific work environments, such as hospitals, banks, colleges, retail stores, or local government. For instance, people working in an educational setting might use a prompt to start the exercise such as

It seems to me like my class load is heavier than the other people in this department.

I've just about had it with the kids in my class.

How come there are more students in my class than in any other class in this school?"

There is no substitute for actual practice and experience with active listening. Most communities have counseling or mental health workers that can provide this type of training for organizations.

If supervisors have had some active listening training and experience, it may be useful to reinforce their skills with a self-administered survey such as the LaMonica Empathy Profile, published by XICOM. Dr. Elaine LaMonica developed this survey out of her work in counseling and nursing education. This survey provides people with feedback regarding five modes or areas of strength in listening. It provides an excellent tool for reinforcing the active listening concepts and leads people to strengthen their range of listening abilities.

Managing Conflict

Autocratic behavior may have been an effective way for supervisors to avoid conflict with their employees. When employees are conditioned to be submissive, some conflict will be avoided. On the other hand, autocracy often creates resentment and leads to smoldering resistance and conflict over control.

Empowering leaders come to understand that conflict is a normal part of any team effort. Each individual has a different type of personality, different knowledge, and different experiences. It is perfectly normal for people to be in conflict.

Supervisors need an opportunity to learn a bit of conflict theory and learn about their own style of handling conflict. There are several good conflict style instruments available to help people learn how they typically deal with conflict. This self-awareness allows people to perform better in conflict situations, which normally arise in an organization. Empowering leadership allows conflicts over issues and personalities to be resolved instead of denied by engaging people in dialogue and discussion. Conflict over control tends to disappear.

The instruction on conflict resolution for the team leaders should include a self-assessment tool that allows an individual to get feedback regarding his or her approach to dealing with conflict, such as the *Thomas-Kilman Conflict Mode Instrument,* published by XICOM. If necessary, the new team leader will be able to use this type of instrument with all the team members as a way to help the team resolve issues where the team is having problems dealing with conflict styles.

If an instrument such as the *Thomas-Kilman Conflict Mode Instrument* is used, it is important to offer suggestions to participants to help them consider how to modify their style to achieve a more collaborative approach to conflict resolution that is vital to most team situations. Self-assessment instruments often will give feedback, but will couch it in language that reassures people that there are both strengths and weaknesses to any style. Although this may be comforting and helps overcome denial of the feedback, people need suggestions as to what specific actions they might take to improve their ability to lead in an empowering manner.

Those whose scores indicate a tendency to approach conflict from a "competing" perspective need to

- Work on recognizing other peoples' interests.
- Ask themselves what they can learn from a conflict situation.
- Ask people how they feel about the alternatives.
- Define what others need to "win."

Those whose scores suggest that they tend to avoid conflict need to

- Ask people to define and recognize their differences.
- Ask people to define a "win." Insist on "win-win" answers.
- Make a list of their own conflicts, prioritize the list, and then address each issue with a plan.

People whose feedback suggests that they will tend to accommodate the needs of others at their own expense should

- Define everyone's objectives in a conflict situation.
- Insist on dialogue and agreement on how to weigh the merits of the objectives people want to achieve.
- Encourage brainstorming of options.
- Make sure that everyone in the team participates in discussions.

For more advanced training on resolving conflicts, people who want to learn to become effective empowering leaders should study the suggestions from the Harvard Negotiation Project, published by Roger Fisher and William Ury in their book, *Getting to Yes*.

Establishing Measures

To function as empowering leaders, supervisors need to involve the people in their team in identifying what activities should be measured by the team. The types of measures needed in an effective organization will be detailed in Chapter 4, and include the idea of measures of internal and external indicators. The leader's role is to ensure that the measures are established in a participative manner, ensure there is consensus or at least agreement to the measures, and ensure that the measures are posted and tracked in a location where all the team members can see the results. Indicators should be one of the topics in the regular team meeting.

Group Decision Making

Although it is certainly easier for one person to make some decisions, the quality of the decision making is usually improved when a team participates in the process. Implementation of decisions is almost always easier if everyone had an opportunity to share in the decision making. A basic truism of human behavior, stated throughout this book, is that those who create tend to support, and an empowering leader must understand this concept and use it every day.

Empowering leaders need to know how to guide their team in a rational decision-making process. The objectives to be accomplished by the the decision need to be agreed on by everyone before considering the various alternatives. Even when a decision is made, the whole group should pause to identify the things that could go wrong with the decision and develop contingency plans.

In some cases, team leaders will need to know how to lead a team in brainstorming and then in some form of voting. Some teams use colored dots, which are placed beside brainstorming ideas to select the best ideas to implement. Others use a method for voting by placing weighted scores by ideas as in the nominal group technique covered in Chapter 5. There are many methods that work. The new empowering leader needs to know at least one of them.

In general, group decision making should be done on a consensus basis, which means that all team members can live with at least 70 percent of what is agreed on at any time. Teams want to avoid enacting decisions that give individual members significant heartburn.

Teaching Skills

Empowering leaders do not need the teaching skills associated with non-participative learning. There is no need for lecturing or pouring knowledge into someone's head. Instead, empowering leaders need to awaken to the realization that we are all learning every day. When a team decides to improve a situation, it embarks on what Juran called the diagnostic journey, which is a learning process. The famed Shewhart cycle was advanced by the educator, John Dewey, over seventy years ago as a fundamental approach to learning about the world around us. Educators call it *action research*, because it involves people in learning by taking actions in the world in which they live, as illustrated in Figure 3.5.

The teaching skills for action research are skills related to facilitate group learning. These skills include the ability to pose questions in a manner that encourages creative thinking, the ability to guide a team in collecting data, the ability to encourage dialogue, and the knack for synthesizing ideas.

Teaching Skills For Action Research
• Pose questions to encourage creative thinking.

Figure 3.5
Action Research Cycle

Action Research Cycle

Pose Questions
Based on the
Situation

People Assess
the Results of
Their Actions

Involve People
in Researching
Their Situation

People in the Situation
Create Theories for
Change and
Implement Their Ideas

JD109

- Guide the team in collecting data.
- Encourage dialogue.
- Synthesize ideas.

Posing Questions

The posing of a question is often the opening of the door to knowledge. How a question is asked will frame the matter in a certain way that will influence the manner in which people think about the issue. In many situations, the vital question to be posed will focus the group on the objective(s) to be achieved.

Another valuable line of questioning involves what the Japanese call "The Five Whys," which is a right-brain approach to root cause analysis. The question "Why?" should be repeated to the group to encourage people to peel back the layers of an issue and to face the root cause. In many cases, meaningful change in a system can only come about by identifying root causes of situations and taking actions to change the system at its foundations.

Collecting Data

The empowering leader must be well aware of the variety of tools available for collecting data that are covered in Chapter 4. It is the empowering leader's role to suggest using various tools, depending on the situation. However, it is *not* the empowering leader's role to gather the data *for* the group and to give them the information. This type of action may be expeditious at the moment, but will foster endullment and dependency.

Encourage Dialogue

The empowering leaders has the responsibility for ensuring that all the team members are engaged in the team's dialogue. This often means calling specifically on the quiet members of the team to ensure that their voice is heard. New members may be reluctant to express their opinions. People who disagree may remain silent, withholding important information or perspectives because they are afraid to "rock the boat." As a teacher, the leader should be acquainted with Irving Janis's work on the "group think" phenomenon.

Synthesize Ideas

Groups cannot take forever exploring options and brainstorming ideas. At some point, an issue needs to be brought to closure. This often means the leader must synthesize, or pull together and summarize, the group's decisions into a cohesive whole. The synthesizing process may only involve restating what has been stated in the dialogue process, or it may entail the blending of competing ideas into a new course of action that provides a consensus for the group. The timing for offering a synthesis, and the ability to create a synthesis, can only be developed through experience.

EMPOWERMENT AND EDUCATION

Empowering leaders quickly appreciate the strong link between education and empowerment. All learning influences the political realities of our environment, and the political environment influences all learning. The Italian social thinker, Antonio Gramsci, observed that educational processes in a nation are based on the values of whatever group provides leadership to the state. The social structures of the nation, such as its educational system, then serve to perpetuate the values of the dominant group. How a nation organizes its production capacity depends on the consciousness of the people as well. It will be incongruent to be teaching empowered decision making in school systems and workplaces if the schools and workplaces are designed to support autocratic control.

Because of the strong link between empowerment and education, a knowledgeable workforce is ready for empowerment and needs empowerment to be satisfied. A workforce without knowledge needs education before empowerment. Of course, the best way to prevent empowerment is to deny education, just as the best way to oppress a people is to deny them schools, literacy, and access to information that can set them free.

The opposite condition of empowerment in today's workplace is usually not oppression, but rather the condition known as endullment. Endullment is the dulling of peoples' minds as a result of their nonparticipation. It occurs in schools and it happens at work. Endullment leads to low motivation, poor attendance, refusal to cooperate to improve the system, and defeatism. Endullment conditions people to be apathetic about the world around them, whether it be in a slum, a factory, or any other work setting.

Team-building Skills

There are many different approaches to team building. Some approaches focus on developing greater understanding of the unique contributions that each team member can make to the team, causing people to value differences and diversity. Other team-building approaches focus on helping people understand why it is important for the team to work together, or on how to establish or increase the trust among the team members. Still other team-building efforts focus on helping team members appreciate the critical role of communication within teams and to explore their own communication styles in order to improve their group's dynamics.

An excellent and inexpensive tool for building cohesion within a team is the *I Speak Your Language* instrument, published by Drake, Beam, and Morin. This instrument is a self-assessment tool that gives people quick feedback regarding how they tend to relate to other people under normal conditions and under stress. It is important for team leaders to have self-awareness of their personality styles. Team leaders who are familiar with this type of instrument can also use it with their team members as a team-building exercise. An alternate approach is to use a more elaborate assessment instrument, such as Wilson Learning's Managing Interpersonal Relations, or the Myers-Briggs Personality Indicator, both of which require a certified facilitator to administer and interpret.

The *I Speak Your Language* instrument gives people feedback based on a model of four personality types: sensors, thinkers, feelers, and intuitors.

People whose scores indicate a tendency toward the sensor area will tend to value factual information, want to be in control in situations, have a focus on achieving results and value getting to the bottom line and bringing issues to closure. People with these traits will want to have clearly defined boundaries in which to work. The sensor's preferred communication style is often to tell people what needs to be done.

Other people will have scores indicating a tendency to act as a feeler, being comfortable with involving people in discussions, and often preferring communication based on asking others for their thoughts and feelings. People with this style are often caring, able to listen, and want people to be comfortable within their boundaries. Feelers will often consider focus groups to be an ideal way to "pulse" the organization, which is a concept they tend to value.

The thinker style values information, the exploration and consideration of options, the collection and analysis of data, and the use of data and evidence for rational decision making. People whose scores indicate a strength in this area often appreciate having clear boundaries, as long as the boundaries make sense.

Some people have scores on the "I Speak" exercise that indicate they are intuitors. The intuitors enjoy the ability to be creative, to invent new options, to be energetic and opinionated. Intuitors will reluctantly accept boundaries, but prefer them to be broad, if they must exist.

A work group is usually strengthened by having people with a variety of personality types, even though their differences may create conflict and cause people to get on each others' nerves. Groups need sensors to bring issues to closure. Feelers help keep the group aware of how its actions impact others and can help the group remain cohesive. Thinkers push the group to make decisions based on data, and keep the group from making premature decisions. The intuitors encourage creativity and challenge the group to move beyond the status quo. When a type is missing, the group can suffer.

When a sensor seeks to be an empowering leader, he or she often needs to practice patience, practice asking questions instead of telling, ask people to set their own deadlines, and be careful not to over praise the other sensors in the group.

When a feeler is in the leadership position, he or she will enjoy the human interaction. However, feelers need to listen to the sensor's need for closure and the thinker's need for information. Feelers need to openly discuss conflict and not deny its existence.

When thinkers are providing leadership, they often need to focus on people's feelings and to encourage people to use right-brain tools such as brainstorming. The thinkers need to balance their analytical strengths by asking making sure there are deadlines on issues. The thinkers, feelers, and sensors need to be careful not to marginalize the sometimes outspoken, but creative participation of the intuitors.

Intuitors who seek to be empowering leaders need to give the thinkers the time they need to process information. Feelers need to be given the time to feel confident of the "pulse" of the organization, too. Intuitors must make a point to not overwhelm the team by generating too many possibilities and options. The intuitor will encourage brainstorming, but he or she should always go last in the process. The other tools for group process that are more data oriented must not be neglected. Intuitors must remind themselves to check the boundaries to ensure that they are being followed. Intuitors like the idea of leading, but may find it limits their creative energies.

Different organization will need to work on different issues to build teams. In some cases, people can benefit greatly by watching and discussing the video series by Dr. Morris Massey, *What You Are Is Where You Were* to appreciate and overcome their differences.

An empowering leaders does not have to be an organizational development expert, with a bag full of dozens of team-building tricks. She or he needs only a few tools that fit the culture of the organization and are comfortable and easy to use. There are plenty of books and videotapes that can be used as resources in this particular skill area.

Setting the Boundaries

It is very important for the empowering leader to clarify the work group's initial boundaries. Boundary definition needs to be established by the management and understood by the team leader and all the team members. Boundaries differ from one workplace to another, but generally all groups have boundaries regarding obeying laws that apply to the workplace. Health, safety, and environmental regulations create boundaries within which teams must work. Budget restrictions often create boundaries. The boundaries give the team members a clear understanding of what they can and cannot do.

New employees, or newly formed teams, may need to have tighter boundaries than experienced people or seasoned teams require. A new person needs some time and more coaching to be able to work in a mature manner. New teams often need a high degree of initial coaching to work out successful patterns of planning, communication, and review of performance.

Different organizations will have varying ranges of boundaries when it comes to human resources policies. Some organizations allow empowered teams to conduct their own performance appraisals, interview and hire team members, and conduct their own discipline. Other organizations reserve these functions to the human resources group. Newly formed teams will need adequate time to master the control of their internal work functions before they are given the added responsibility of making human resources decisions.

Creating an Implementation Plan

The team leader who is going to lead in a participative manner must gain the consent of the people about to be "liberated." This is often a slow process, since an endulled workforce may be comfortable with its situation, even if the organization is going out of business.

Empowerment is not something management does *to* people, and this point needs to be stressed with the team leaders. Empowerment is a process in which people have to participate in defining and creating their own liberation. When people are not ready to accept the responsibility of becoming empowered, there must be an educational process to set the stage for change.

When the climate is right for change, it is ideal to involve people in planning the change process. A plan is important because in spite of everyone's best efforts, there will be some leaders who want to hold on to their comfortable autocratic behavior. The plan forces the organization to confront this situation. People must be challenged to lead in an empowering manner, participate as an empowered team member, or find some isolated task where they do not need to work with others. Tools, such as performance dialogue, can be used to reinforce the desired change in the organization's culture.

Mentors Can Help

In additional to providing structured training for supervisors, it helps to also develop a cadre of people who have already made the transition from endulling to empowering leadership to facilitate the change process.

These individuals can serve as coaches and mentors to ensure that behavioral changes really take place and can guide leaders in dealing with the emotional challenges created by new leadership styles.

There are two groups of people who make natural mentors for this transition process. One group consists of former supervisors who have become empowering team leaders and who can speak from direct experience. The second group consists of middle managers to whom the team leaders will report.

Utilizing former supervisors who have become empowering team leaders offers many benefits. First, these people have high credibility because they have already made the transition and can relate to all the concerns that supervisors may have. This mentor can speak with personal conviction regarding the fears and reservations that supervisors may have about changing their leadership style. This mentor will have personal examples of what worked for him or her in making the transition, and has the personal credibility to argue on behalf of making the change.

If middle managers are used as the mentors, they must clearly be people who are acknowledged as empowerment champions. If these mentors do not have high credibility as supporters of empowerment, it will be a greater challenge for them to play the role of mentor. People who are clearly empowerment champions and who are in middle management will have credibility in that they can assure people that the organization really will support the transition process. As empowerment champions, they have already demonstrated their willingness and ability to lead through creating empowering situations, so they will have personal credibility as a mentor.

To mentor new team leaders, there are several specific actions that need to be taken. First, the mentor should be fully aware of the content of the training that is provided to the supervisors to help them transition to being a team leader. With the content of the training in mind, the mentor needs to set up a one-on-one meeting. In this meeting, the mentor should ask the new team leader to share his or her plan for establishing team meetings and setting up performance indicators. The mentor should ask the team leader to identify the difficulties he or she anticipates with empowering this specific work group, and what actions are planned to mitigate these concerns.

The mentor should then arrange to sit in on one of the team's meetings within a month of the training for the team leader. The mentor should check to ensure that the meetings are occurring on a regular basis. The mentor needs to observe whether or not the meetings are involving the whole team, or if one or two people (possibly the team leader) are dominating the meeting. The mentor should check to ensure that performance indicators are in place and that the team members buy in to their use.

After observing a team meeting, the mentor needs to arrange a follow-up meeting with the team leader. The mentor should give the team leader feedback regarding what was observed. Where the mentor sees problems, he or she should ask the team leader what should be done to improve the situation. Please note that it is not the mentor's role to tell the team leader what to do. Instead, the mentor serves as a source of feedback and dialogue for the team leader.

The mentor should schedule a follow-up observation of the team within two to three months. Again, the mentor observes whether or not the team meetings are occurring, the use of performance indicators, and the dynamics of the group. The mentor should give his or her observations to the team leader after the meeting.

CREATING A SUPPORT GROUP FOR TEAM LEADERS

Making the transition from autocrat or benevolent autocrat to participative or democratic leader requires time to learn and adapt to new patterns of thinking and behavior. No one should believe that simply sending supervisors to a training program on participative leadership engenders meaningful change in those supervisors. Even when the supervisor cognitively endorses a highly participative style, old patterns of behavior can inhibit walking the talk.

The empowerment champions may find that the leaders in the organization need to have a vehicle for ongoing dialogue and learning to support the transition process, in addition to having coaches in the organization. A leadership discussion group that meets regularly can provide leaders with a forum for asking questions, comparing notes, and expressing concerns about how their particular leadership experience is developing. A member of the empowerment champions can serve as the initial chairperson for this committee.

If an organization has provided training on participative leadership, the person who conducted the training would be a good resource to include in the leadership discussion group. This person can serve as the focal point for questions and review of issues. However, the "educator" in this setting needs to avoid providing all of the answers, and instead, involve all of the leaders in exchanging their ideas and their knowledge about how to handle problems. The leadership discussion group needs to be an empowering forum for education, not an endulling meeting where people passively listen to an "expert."

In designing the overall change process for an organization, the planners should remember that change occurs gradually, and the new behaviors need to be reinforced. Different people have differing modes of learning. Some learn by reading, some by watching, some by discussing, and some by doing. Those who learn by doing and discussing will be well served by participating in a leadership discussion group.

In most cases, the change process in an organization requires months or years to perfect. An ongoing leadership discussion group offers the empowerment planning team a forum for testing ideas, explaining changes in the system's reinforcing programs, such as compensation, and provides an extra feedback loop to the planning team to help in identifying modifications that need to be made to the change effort.

APPENDIX:
Opportunities for Praxis

1. Who are the people in your organization that would make good members of an empowerment planning team?

2. What types of training resources are available in your area to help supervisors become democratic leaders?

3. What are your organization's strengths as far as training investments that have already been made that can strengthen the migration to an empowering workplace?

4. Who would serve well as mentors for supervisors in your organization to help them continue to modify their leadership styles?

5. How would you form a leadership discussion group in your organization to create a place for dialogue about empowerment?

4

Education for an Empowered Workforce

Education of a liberating character is a process by which the educator invites learners to recognize and unveil reality critically.

—Paulo Freire, *The Politics of Education*

As the empowerment champions and the empowerment planning team consider the learning needs of the organization's managers and supervisors, initiating seminars and workshops to enable the managers to lead in an empowering manner, consideration must also be given to the educational needs of the workforce.

Anyone who embarks on the challenge of educating and preparing people to work as empowered members in the workplace will be confronted with many interesting and serious questions. One quickly finds that the educational system has not been designed to prepare people to enter into the workforce and be active participants in decision making. For many decades, the educational system has consciously reinforced autocratic methods of learning and behavior that inhibited students' abilities to actively learn and participate in the creation of their own learning process. Now, this is changing in many school systems, as students are more involved in learning how to participate in making decisions that impact their lives.

There are useful insights regarding the type of education that is needed to foster empowered behavior in the workplace that the empowerment planning team can draw on. It would be wise to start the planning of workforce education by examining these observations. One of the first systematic observations was offered by Leland Bradford and Ronald Lippitt in 1945. They noticed that to be successful, a supervisor must tailor his or her approach to participation on the needs of the specific group he or she is leading.

> Every supervisor must realize that he starts from where the group is. If the group has been accustomed to rigid supervisory control, with no opportunity for initiative or responsibility, to give complete responsibility in the beginning would only result in a laissez-faire situation. In such cases responsibility must be gradually extended, with more careful encouragement and leadership given to the employees.

Bradford and Lippitt's observations suggest that rather than a single approach to empowering a work group, the leader must customize the approach to offering people empowerment, based upon the ability and the maturity of the group members.

Also writing in 1945, Kurt Lewin observed that empowerment requires a learning style of leadership and "followership" that are different from the roles found in autocracy.

> Establishing democracy in a group implies an active education: the democratic followers must learn to play a role which implies, among other things, a fair share of responsibility toward the group, and a sensitivity to other people's feelings.

The learning of empowered behaviors cannot be accomplished through autocratic means, Lewin insisted. "These principles might be clarified by lecture, but they can be learned, finally, only by democratic living."

Lewin's observations have been echoed more recently by Marvin Weisbord, who has been active in introducing empowering practices into the workplace. Weisbord noted that learning plays a vital part in achieving empowerment. However, he has also observed that "each time people are sent to classes without vehicles for participating in policy, procedure, strategy, goal setting and work design, they rightfully feel conned."

Based on Lewin and Weisbord's observations, the empowerment planning team can surmise that empowerment requires an educational plan that is coupled with changes that allow people to experience both the stress and benefits of empowerment. Skills that enable empowerment cannot be taught in the normal classroom lecture style. These enabling behaviors will require highly participative workshop settings and on-the-job praxis.

Seven Step Path to Empowerment
1. Create champions.
2. Involve people in planning the change.
3. Create team leaders.

➤ *4. Educate the workforce.*
  5. Change the support system.
  6. Practice consensus decision making.
  7. Involve people in strategic and tactical planning.

There are five broad areas in which the workforce will need education and training, over time, to successfully participate in running their organization. The specific content of these areas depends on the mission of the organization and the type of work that people perform. The five areas are Vocational Skills, Business Skills, Process Skills, Interpersonal Skills, and Political skills shown in Table 4.1.

VOCATIONAL

To be effective, people need the proper vocational skills and knowledge necessary for their task functions in the organization. The lack of vocation skills contributes to the creation of an endulling work environment, but the presence of vocational skills alone does not make an environment empowering. Vocational skills are necessary, along with other interlocking skills, to create the empowering work environment.

The types of vocational skills needed are obviously going to depend on the type of work being performed. What needs to be addressed at this point is a quick method for identifying the necessary vocational skills, if this has not already been done in the organization.

There are basically two approaches. The first approach is rather simple. Ask each person to list the jobs they perform, and beside each job, write down what skill or special information is needed. Then, determine if this skill or knowledge is a standard part of the educational curriculum that a person in this position would already know, or see if there is special training needed. For example, a nurse in a doctor's office might be expected to perform dozens of task that would have been taught in the nurse's school training. However, if the office has added a new piece of equipment, there

Table 4.1
Areas of Workforce Education Needs

Areas of Education	Content
Vocational	Specific to the business
Business	Financial and performance indicators
Process	Logic diagrams and decision-making tools
Interpersonal	Communications and conflict management
Political	Reflective practice, strategic planning, and force field analysis

may need to be special training on how it is operated. The same is true for many different work areas.

If a few cases (such as the operation of complex and hazardous systems), it will be worth the time and investment to conduct a more detailed analysis of the work being performed (which is the second approach), since the tasks may not be a part of any expected curriculum of study that a person would pick up in school. For instance, a control room operator at a power station will have many job-specific functions that would not be covered in a technical school or college. In this case, the operator's job should be described in detail, and each task should be assessed to determine the necessary knowledge and skills. A detailed lesson plan should be created, and training provided that ensures the employee has the knowledge and skills. The employees who now perform these tasks should be involved in defining the technical skills, developing and reviewing the training, and in training new employees.

Many organizations are addressing the training issue through the use of videotape and computer interactive training. If vocational training can be placed on videotape or on a personal computer, then the employee can refer to the training when needed, or can review the information at times that are convenient to the employee. Where possible, videotape and computer training should use actual employees to give the content of the presentation.

Teaching vocational skills can be done in either an empowering or an endulling manner. Empowering vocational education allows people to

Figure 4.1
An Empowering Budget Cycle

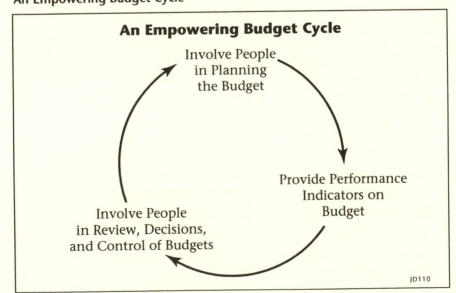

spend as much or as little time to learn a skill as each individual requires. Specific tasks are taught, but the theory behind the tasks is also made available. Empowering vocational education emphasizes learning to perform work, often using simulations, exercises, or drills that allow participants to critique their own performance. Table 4.2 compares the empowering and endulling approaches to vocational education.

Endulling vocational education offers "one-size-fits-all" curriculum, often based on lecture, with an emphasis on passing tests. In order to assure that people can pass the tests, instructors resort to teaching to the specific test content. Learning modules are often locked into required lengths of time, regardless of the learners' knowledge base. Learners quickly find themselves in an endulling environment, often reminiscent of poorly led high school classes.

BUSINESS

The endulling organization does not take the time to educate people on the economic realities of the business. Team members are not involved in budgeting or reviewing budget information, and the cost of operating the work group is often an undiscussed issue. Therefore, it should come as no surprise when endulling organizations overspend budgets and cannot control costs.

Most people in the workplace handle their own budgets and financial accounts at home. They manage to file their tax forms, and some serve in private organizations or civic groups that handle sizable amounts of money.

Table 4.2
Empowering versus Endulling Approaches to Teaching Vocational Skills

Empowering	Endulling
Content based on review of actual job needs.	Content based on "expert's" opinions.
Emphasis on learning through exercises and simulations.	Emphasis on lectures.
Length of training based on each learner's need.	Length of training based on "expert's" opinion or a rule.
Provides challenging exercises.	Teaches to the test.
Participants can critique the learning process.	No opportunity for critique.

However, in the workplace, there often appears to be a reluctance to involve people in the financial situation, while at the same time, there is a tendency to complain about employees who do not control costs.

If people in a work organization are to be cost conscious, customer oriented, and empowered, they must be involved in the budget cycle, shown in Figure 4.1. Involving people in the budgeting process creates a challenge and opportunity for both the managers and the people in the workplace. For the managers, the challenge is to be open at the front of the cycle and to give people an opportunity to plan their part of the budget, and then to assure that they receive feedback as the cycle progresses. For the people, the challenge is to own up to the budget information and take responsibility for controlling their part of the budget.

Empowering leaders will begin the budget cycle by calling their teams together and defining the boundaries for budgeting. The boundary may be that each time's budget cannot exceed some amount of money that the leader has established. Or perhaps the amount of money in the budget depends on revenues the team brings in. In either case, the team members need to understand what the rules are.

As much as possible, the leader should give team members latitude in deciding how and when to spend their money, as long as they stay within their boundaries. However, if it is important to minimize expenditures during the year, people need to be told that minimizing expenses is something they should try to do. If, on the other hand, it is better to spend all of the budget for whatever is needed, then that condition should also be explained.

A set of performance indicators related to the budget needs to be established where everyone can see what is going on. These indicators might show the breakdown of the categories of the budget and would indicate the amount spent each day, week, or month. If the organization generates revenues, then the incoming funds might also be appropriate for the team to see. Team members need to recognize that some or all of this information might be sensitive and not for sharing with customers or competitors.

The review of budgets and other data related to cost control should be a part of the regular agenda of the team. Other related data might include information on the amount of overtime being worked by the team members and the absenteeism statistics for the team. With this information, team members will be able to tell if they are within bounds and profitable, or out of bounds and being too costly to the organization.

PROCESS SKILLS

Organizations that have already invested in teaching the quality tools to most of their people are well positioned for empowerment, since the quality tools are vital process skills. If an organization has not yet taught its people the quality process skills, then these need to be covered in a brief workshop that illustrates how the tools have been utilized in the specific environment of that organization. Generic examples are of little value. The teaching materials must be customized to the specific environment to be fully understood and accepted. The most vital process skills are flow charting, cause enumeration, process classification, and the Pareto diagram.

Flow Charting

Flow diagrams allow us to visually define how a work process is performed. Such diagrams can show how the work is done in its proper sequence of steps. Boxes are used to indicate steps where work is done and diamonds are used to indicate where decisions are made. Use lines to connect the boxes, with arrows to show the flow of information or materials.

Flow diagrams can be used to define the process and to identify which steps are value added and which steps add only cost. These diagrams show interfaces between organizations where communications might break down and help determine areas for which a team might need to collect data and use statistical control charts.

One specific value of the flow diagram is its use in measuring rework. The diagram will show the path work must take when it requires rework. One can set up a mechanism to count the number of times a product goes around in a loop before it makes it out of the process flow.

The construction of a flow diagram is the first step in any form of cycle-time reduction. The diagram allows people to study the effectiveness of the "as is" process. As a diagnostic tool, a flow chart helps improve the communication within a team by providing a common point of reference for all team members to see regarding the process they are improving.

Flow diagrams not only help in diagnosing how a system works but also make a wonderful training tool. New people in the organization can be given a flow diagram that illustrates how an entire process works so that they can see how their specific work fits into the big picture. Without understanding the entire process, people may not recognize the importance of their part of the work or the implications if they change the system or make a mistake.

A common example of the flow diagram (Figure 4.2) can be seen in this example of mowing the lawn. First comes the decision to mow or not, based on the weather. Then come the preliminary steps to prepare to mow. Failure to pick up sticks before mowing can cause damage to the mower or frequent pauses in the mowing work. After the mowing, comes the inspection and possibly rework. Rework adds no value to the process, only additional costs. This illustration should make the point that any process can be flow charted. The information gained by flow charting can lead to significant reduction in re-work and errors, cost savings for the organization, and improvements in the products and services provided to customers.

The Cause Enumeration Diagram

Cause enumeration diagrams help teams to identify the possible causes that may be contributing to problems that the team members are experiencing. The diagram enables people to visualize the relationship between the possible causes and the effect being experienced.

Create this diagram by first showing the effect in a box on the right side of your page. Then draw a center line running to the box, with branch lines that have major headings of problem categories. Next comes deciding what the major categories will be that are appropriate for the issue at hand. Often, categories such as people, procedures, materials, equipment, and the environment work very well. Then, identify the possible causes that might lead to the effect.

The Cause Enumeration diagram does not give conclusive evidence of the cause of a problem. Rather, it serves to display the factors related to a problem and allows people to build a common perception. The interrelationship of factors can be seen by everyone.

As an example, consider the causes that lead to a successful or unsuccessful fishing trip, shown in Figure 4.3. There are definitely categories of factors that will impact the outcome, such as the environment, people, the process used, the equipment, and materials. In each category, one can

Figure 4.2
Flow Diagram

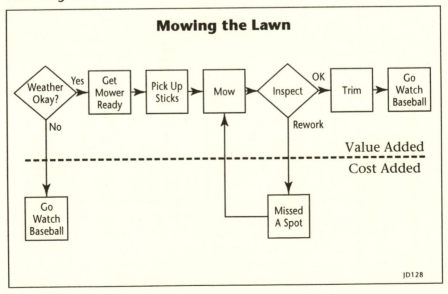

Figure 4.3
Cause Enumeration Diagram

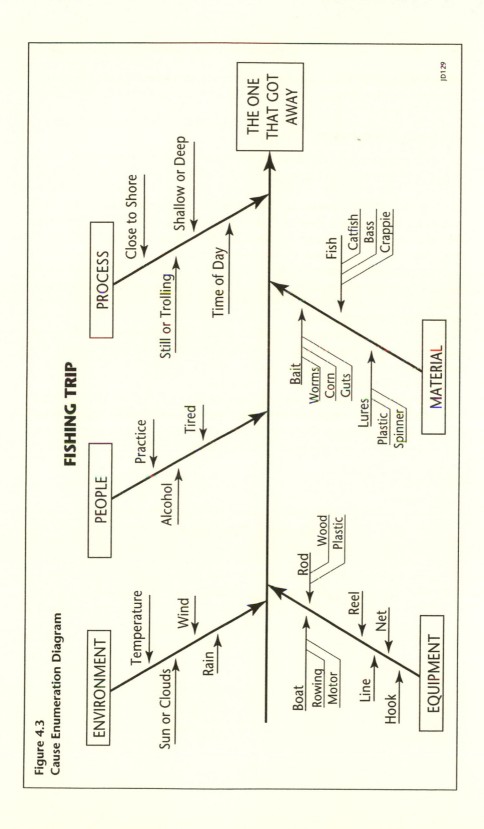

enumerate factors that will influence the outcome.

This diagram can be used to fix a problem or to improve a process. One may decide to try to improve the process by focusing in the materials area and switching bait. Or, one may decide that the equipment needs upgrading and buy a new boat.

Process Classification Diagrams

The Process classification diagram combines the techniques of the flow diagram and the cause enumeration diagram. The process flow is identified and then causes of problems are noted as they occur in the steps of the process.

To prepare this diagram, first identify the problem or effect to be located or removed. Next, establish the work flow by putting the steps into their proper sequence, as in the flow diagram. Then identify the possible causes of the problem or affect by brainstorming. Keep in mind that problems that are visually seen at one step in a process are often caused by events in an earlier step. For example, if the effect one is seeking is to enjoy a football game, there are many steps in the process and many factors that could impact each step (Figure 4.4). In the process flow, one needs to pack to go to the game, park the car, buy tickets, and get something to eat before the game can be truly savored. At each step in the process there are several factors to consider.

The Pareto Diagram

Dr. Joseph Juran took the observations of the Italian economist, Vilfredo Pareto, regarding the distribution of wealth in society and developed a general principle that most events are caused by a small number of factors. The small number of important items were called the "Vital Few" by Juran. The many items that occur that do not impact the situation much were called the "Trivial Many" by Dr. Juran.

For instance, there are only a few billionaires, but they control a great deal of money. There are many people who make minimum wage, but even when you add them all together, they do not have as much economic clout as the few billionaires.

A Pareto diagram is a tool that allows people to arrange data in the form of a chart to compare the relative significance of events or costs. There are five common steps to preparing a Pareto diagram:

1. Decide which data should be shown in the chart.
2. Decide on the time period for collecting data.
3. Collect your data on a worksheet, from budgets or other sources.

Figure 4.4
Process Classification Diagram

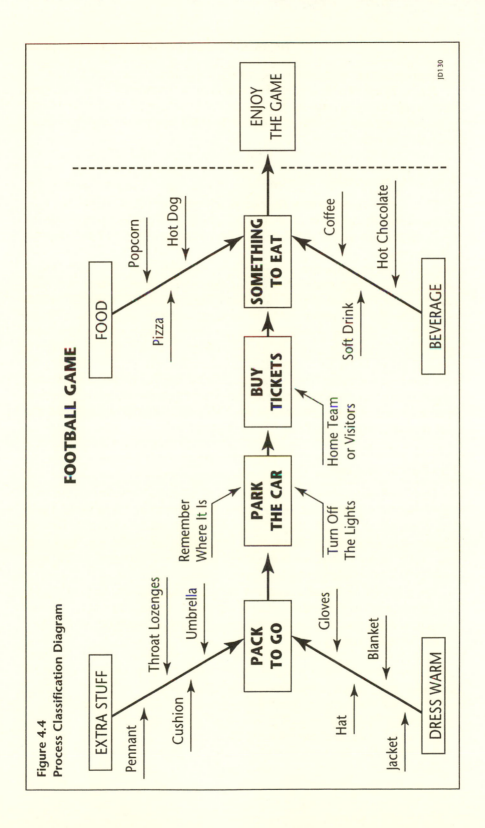

FOOTBALL GAME

ENJOY THE GAME

JD130

4. Construct the Pareto diagram from the data you collected.
   Arrange the data cells in descending order from the left
   of the graph.
5. Add information to make your chart readable to other people.

For instance, a coach might want to determine which players on a basketball team make the greatest contribution in terms of points scored during a game. A Pareto diagram (Figure 4.5) provides a quick method to display the data that allows for easy interpretation of the information.

There are many other quality-related tools that may benefit employees. Organizations must trade off the cost of investing in education people to use these tools with the likelihood that the tools can actually be applied in the specific work area. In most cases, it makes sense to train a team leader or process facilitator and allow them to determine which additional tools should be taught, such as cycle-time reduction, data matrices, run charts, and control charts.

INTERPERSONAL SKILLS

Although it is essential for people to have the technical, budget, and process skills to collect data and determine how well the team is performing, it is also vital that people be able to work and communicate effectively together. In general, people in the workplace need training in several areas of interpersonal skills to effectively work in an empowered manner. These

Figure 4.5
Pareto Diagram

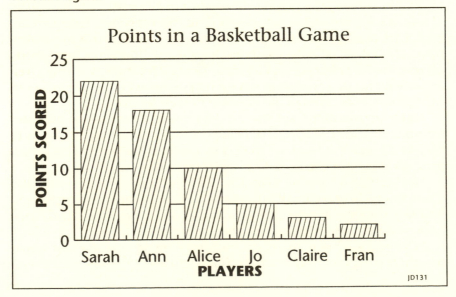

areas of education include some form of personality assessment, listening skills, meeting management skills, and an understanding of conflict resolution. All of these can be covered in a short workshop offered by an internal training person, or can be obtained through community college or other social agencies in many communities.

Interpersonal Skills Training
- Personality Assessment
- Listening Skills
- Meeting Management
- Conflict Resolution

Personality Assessment

There are a variety of ways to provide people with the personality assessment feedback that will help them understand their own unique attributes. The point of the type of feedback is to help people understand that other people will have different personality styles and that these differences are a normal part of the workplace. This feedback helps people accept and value the diversity of styles at work and fosters an understanding and collaborative approach.

Organizations can invest a small amount of time or a large amount of time in this area. For small time investments, the *I Speak Your Language* self- evaluation instrument offered by Drake-Beam-Morrin will give people useful feedback in about an hour's time, with discussion by a leader who can interpret the results. The *I Speak* instrument relies wholly on the participant's answers to questions, so there is no feedback regarding how other people perceive his or her behavior.

Wilson Learning Corporation offers a personality assessment tool called *Managing Interpersonal Relations,* or MIR. The MIR assessment relies on feedback from other people who are coworkers for its data. With this instrument, the individual gains significant insight into how his or her coworkers perceive his or her personality style. The MIR feedback is usually given to participants in a workshop setting with a trained facilitator who can help people work through the meaning of their feedback.

Many organizations opt for the Myers-Briggs Personality Indicator instrument. The Myers-Briggs approach offers the advantage that it is to only be administered and interpreted by a trained facilitator. This instrument gives detailed feedback in a workshop setting.

Stephen Covey's workshop on *The 7 Habits of Highly Effective People* also offers an excellent feedback instrument. This instrument does not try to establish a personality type, but does offer people very good feedback based on how others around them view their behavior.

Whatever approach an organization may choose, it should be noted that there is a distinct advantage to choosing one of these approaches and using it consistently throughout the organization. If part of the organization uses Myers-Briggs and another group uses MIR, then the ability to discuss these concepts across organizational boundaries is limited. Unfortunately, many organizations adopt these tools in a rather haphazard manner, with little thought about how they can be used in a uniform manner for maximum effect.

Listening Skills

There is a significant body of knowledge about how to enable people to better listen to one another. Most of this knowledge is taught in the social work and counseling fields. Almost any organization can bring in a school counselor or community social worker to conduct a short seminar on listening.

Although the general public may perceive that a counselor's job is to tell troubled people what to do to straighten out their lives, this is a misinformed perception. Most counselors and social workers spend a great deal of time listening to people and asking questions that help people explore their own issues and arrive at their own conclusions.

This same approach to communication will effectively improve communication within organizations and fosters the concept of empowerment. When a person has a problem, coworkers need to be able to listen to the concern and to focus on the factual information and the feelings that the employee is expressing. They do not need to solve the problem for their fellow employee. Instead, they need to be able to ask their coworker for his or her ideas as to how the issue should be resolved, within the boundaries that are available.

This general field of communication theory is called *active listening,* and was developed by Carl Rogers. Most psychologists, social workers, and counselors have been trained in this field. Many social agencies, such as telephone crisis centers, offer training in this methodology. It will not be hard to find someone in your community who can teach this skill in a short workshop.

Running Meetings

A lot of the communication that needs to occur within an empowered work team will take place in the format of a meeting. Team members need some exposure to the methods of running effective meetings so that they will be aware of their own behaviors and be able to contribute to a successful meeting. The guidelines for running meetings are relatively simple and can be picked up in many different books.

What is not widely perceived about meetings, and what impacts the nature of a meeting from the perspective of empowering people, is the variety of objectives that a meeting can serve. There are at least seven different types of process that can be worked within the setting of a meeting. Meetings can be used to explore opportunities and concerns, to develop strategic and tactical plans, to make decisions, to solve problems, to update people on the status of situations, or to simply share information.

Empowering meetings will work all seven processes, as they are appropriate for the situation. Endulling meetings concentrate on the last two processes, updating and sharing, so that people tend to be passive listeners in the meeting, rather than being active players.

Seven Processes of Meetings
1. Exploration of opportunities and concerns
2. Planning (strategic and tactical)
3. Decision making
4. Problem solving
5. Systems improvement
6. Status updates
7. Information sharing

When boundaries are tightly drawn around a team, meetings will tend to only involve the last two processes. As boundaries are expanded to foster empowerment, the other processes begin to be utilized in meetings. The odds are pretty good that people in the team have been engaged in using these other processes in other settings, so they may be familiar with the workings. What may need to be stated to everyone, however, is the point at which the meeting shifts from one process into another.

Exploration Of Opportunities and Concerns

In this process, participants brainstorm issues that are of concern to the team, or opportunities that the team needs to pursue. The focus should be on current situations or future possibilities. Team members should identify these opportunities and concerns, and then prioritize them to determine which issues are most important and deserving of immediate action.

The prioritization of issues should take into account which concerns or opportunities have deadlines, which have the greatest impact or opportunity regarding organizational objectives, which concerns may get worse over time, and which opportunities may disappear over time.

Planning

Planning meetings can focus on either strategic or tactical plans. Strategic planning is a whole topic in and of itself, but every team should have its own mission statement and vision of what it wants to become over time.

Most planning in teams is tactical planning. When a team moves into tactical planning, there needs to be a commitment to defining what will be done, by whom, and by when. These plans should be documented, and often should be illustrated with a time plan or Gantt chart that is posted for every team member to see. Most important of all, team members should spend some time identifying what might go wrong with their plan and taking actions to either keep the problems from occurring, or have some mitigating actions already in place.

If teams develop plans that fail due to the lack of questioning about what might go wrong, energy gets wasted placing blame, and there is a lack of trust in one another. Asking each other what can go wrong is a way to watch each other's backs and building camaraderie.

Decision Making

There is so much to be said on this subject that an entire chapter is devoted to it. Please see chapter 6.

Problem Solving

There are dozens of tools and techniques for solving problems and getting to the root causes of problems. The important thing is to provide the team members with a uniform set of tools that they can use. The process tools that are discussed earlier in this chapter are a great set of tools, if everyone has them.

However, there is an important point to remember about problem solving as contrasted with decision making. In decision making, there is a best answer, based on the input of the team, but not necessarily a right answer. Change the team members and you may change the selection of the team. However, in problem solving there is a right answer. Problems are situations where a system is not working the way that it should. Something is causing the system to work improperly, and there will be a precise answer to fixing it.

Systems Improvement

When a team has a meeting to improve a system, the thinking process of the team again changes. In the improvement process, people will review data and brainstorm ideas with the objective of improving a system. There may not be the urgency of problem solving, since nothing is broken. Some teams refuse to enter into systems improvement because they only have time or willingness to spend energy on the broken things that need fixing now. However, competitive position and customer satisfaction in any type of organization are driven by system improvement.

The same tools for process skills suffice for systems improvement. It is important to recognize that the process skills can be used in a variety of ways, such as problem solving and systems improvement.

Status Updates

Status updates are reviews of the performance indicators by the team. The indicators should be in place for the team to monitor its performance to maximize the team's effectiveness. When the team is in the process of status updates, it might quickly shift into a problem-solving process or a systems improvement process. These rapid shifts in thinking process should be recognized by the team members.

Team members will often need at least a few hours of instruction regarding the creation and interpretation of performance indicators, so that the indicators will be useful. Dr. W. Edwards Deming's teachings on collecting and interpreting data would be quite helpful for many teams.

Information Sharing

Although information is not empowering as a stand-alone process in a meeting, the absence of shared information often becomes a point of contention and source of endullment in organizations. How much information should be shared? It works best to give people more than you think they could possibly want, and them allow them to tell you what information they deem to be of little value. Give people the power to decide what they do not need to know. Do not attempt to make that decision for them.

Conflict Resolution

Regarding conflict resolution training for team members, it is usually best to begin by having everyone participate in some sort of personality profile indicator. This feedback allows people to understand their own styles of dealing with people and why other people have styles that are different that may get on their nerves. A bit of group discussion about the team members' different styles can go a long way to dispel the conflicts that are not based on different interests.

A second tool for team members to use to learn more about conflict is the same tool that can be used to help managers deal with conflict, the *Thomas-Kilman Conflict Mode Instrument*. This self-survey gives team members feedback about how they deal with conflict. Self-awareness regarding our own tendencies to perhaps avoid conflict or to thrive on it, can help the team members focus on how the better work in a collaborative, win-win manner.

The third point for helping teams resolve conflict is to buy a copy of *Getting to Yes* by Roger Fisher and William Ury and ask everyone on the team to read it. Have a group discussion about the concept of negotiating based on interests, and ask team members to reflect on how well they actually do this as a group.

In some cases, work groups may build up a long-standing pattern of distrust and conflict within the group. Group members may harbor anger and grudges toward one another. This problem will not go away with empowerment. In fact, empowerment may bring subtle hostility out into the open. In these rare cases, the organization really has only two choices. One choice is to force the people in the group to deal with their problems, using a neutral person, such as a psychologist or counselor, to help them through the problem. The other option is to move people to other assignments or remove them from the workplace altogether. I have witnessed work groups with long-standing severe personnel problems become award-winning teams through the intervention of a professional counselor.

It is important that team members come to accept the perspective that conflict can be a natural and healthy part of the dynamics of a group, when it leads to creative ideas and better ways to accomplish the group's mission. Conflict that deters the group from accomplishing its mission needs to be managed and resolved as quickly as possible.

Some conflicts are sure to occur regarding the definition of the boundaries of the empowered team. As a team matures, it will want to take on more roles and responsibility. At times, teams will push their boundaries, seeking more authority. Empowering managers should recognize this as a natural part of the growth of a team, and should expand the boundaries when they think the team is ready. It is the manager's role to push back and challenge the team when they ask for authority that may be premature.

POLITICAL SKILLS

Whether people like to acknowledge it or not, every organization, whether it is in the private sector, public sector, or the voluntary sector, is endowed with a political system. All organizations are governed by some sort of system that has its norms and rules, consistent with the information on systems theory in Chapter 2.

Endulled employees recognize their organization's political system and are "disfranchised" in that they are not allowed by the system to participate. They have no voice in how decisions are made, so they become docile or resistant to the system.

Empowered employees are aware of their organization's political system and are formally allowed to play in the game. It is very important for everyone to know some basic tools for developing plans and making decisions within the framework of an organization's political system.

Force Field Analysis

The force field analysis is one of the most powerful tools for creating change that encompasses the political realities of an organization. This tool was developed by the social scientist Kurt Lewin in the 1940s and has served as a cornerstone for organizational development practitioners.

Force field analysis allows people to examine their present situation and to consider where they would strategically like to be in the future, where they will be in the future if there are no changes, and the forces in their environment that encourage or resist change.

This tool is best used with a group of employees working together to get a broad interpretation of the political situation. It can be used by a single individual, but the planning value of the tool is enhanced when several people participate. The tool often draws thoughts out into the open that can create serious reflection and learning within the group, or ignite the group into creative ideas and actions.

The steps of force field analysis are

1. First, briefly state the *current* situation.
2. Briefly describe the ideal situation.
3. Identify where the current situation will go if left on its present track.
4. Identify the forces in the environment that are driving change toward your ideal situation.
5. Identify the forces in your environment that are resisting change toward your ideal situation.

In each of these steps, there needs to be some form of brainstorming to get everyone's input and perceptions.

6. Discuss the driving and restraining forces and decide which ones are most critical.
7. For the critical restraining forces, list some possible actions to reduce the effect of these forces.
8. For the critical driving forces, list some possible actions to increase the effect of these forces.
9. Develop an action plan to implement the possible actions that have been identified.

This tool causes people to face the political realities in their organization. Driving and restraining forces may include the names of some individuals or organizations.

Time Lines

Often it is useful to involve a group in creating a time line to develop a common set of perceptions about how a problem or situation has come into being. This exercise brings out information that not everyone in the group may have known, so it serves to create a level playing field at the same time that it creates a form of tribal story that everyone can agree.

For example, in helping an organization plan the next step in an empowerment process, a time line was developed to help new team members understand the path that the organization had been following in the previous years. This gave the experienced members the chance to reflect on their progress and brought the new team members up to speed with the history of the group.

Art for Awareness

Sometimes groups are not really willing to discuss the political reality in which they work, or they appear to be unaware of their political process-es. This situation calls for a process that will help bring issues out into the open in a nonthreatening manner.

One of the best tools for accomplishing this objective is through basic art work. Divide the group or team into small groups of four or five peo-ple and ask each group to draw a picture that will illustrate their work sit-uation. What comes out is often a real eye-opener to the people. They may be willing to put things into a picture that they would never toss out ver-bally for discussion.

These types of images can be used to stimulate discussion about what is going on in an organization. This methodology has been used for many years at the Highlander Center for Research and Education in Tennessee and is a popular tool among adult educators involved in reflective prac-tice.

REIFICATION

When the Brazilian educator, Paulo Freire, was working on literacy train-ing, he found people would sometimes resist learning to read because they could not conceive any notion that their life situation could possibly change. These people lived as peasants in areas where the land and all deci-sion making was controlled by a wealthy few. It had always been this way in their lifetime and in the lifetime of everyone in their community. The possibility of the social condition changing was utterly foreign and beyond their ability to acknowledge.

This total acceptance of the status quo and denial of even the possi-bility of change is known as reification. It is the belief that the current "sys-tem" (which was created by people) cannot be changed by people.

Reification exists in many workplaces and is often at the root of endulling work practices. People hire into autocratic organization and even-tually accept the autocracy as a permanent and unchangeable situation. Small efforts lacking any long-term strategy to involve people will fail and reinforce the belief that nothing can change.

The empowerment planning team must ask itself some potentially embarrassing questions about the level of reification within their organi-zation. The greater the belief that change cannot occur, the more work needs to be done to unfreeze people's thinking.

Reification is acted out in the workplace as apathy. People show little interest in work or creating change because their thinking process has become reified.

The way to overcome reification is through reflective thinking. Use art awareness and role playing to jolt people's thinking. Use benchmarking to expose them to new paradigms of participation. The process is one of consciousness raising, or as Paulo Freire called it, "conscientization." The task is to enable people to become conscious of their situation and their ability to change their situation.

LEARNING/RESOURCE CENTERS

In order to foster empowerment within an organization, a small learning/resource center located where employees can access information will be beneficial. A resource center is a place where people can go to find information, such as books, video tapes, and articles that will help them implement change.

No one can predict when someone in the organization is going to suddenly get turned on and want to start implementing an innovative idea, such as a self-managed team. Resources for implementing innovative ideas need to be readily at hand so that the inspired person can get immediate information on how to proceed. It is a major turn off to tell someone that there is no information on their idea at the moment, but please wait a few weeks until we can get something ordered. In a few weeks, the momentum for change may be lost.

The resource center can be advertised within the organization as a place available for employees for learning how to create change. A "What's New in the Resource Center" item in the company newsletter or bulletin boards can help create a climate conducive to learning and facilitating change.

An effective resource center will contain materials on a variety of topics such as quality improvement, reengineering, managing change, strategic planning, group dynamics, and personal development. Here are a few basic materials to be included in a resource center.

Group dynamics
Knowles, Malcolm. *Introduction to Group Dynamics,* New York: Cambridge Press, 1972.
Planning
Tregoe, Benjamin B. and Zimmerman, John W. *Top Management Strategy,* New York: Simon and Schuster, 1980.
Weisbord, Marvin. *Discovering Common Ground,* San Francisco: Berrett-Koehler, 1992.
Redesigning the workplace
Hammer, Michael and Champy, James. *Reengineering the Corporation,* New York: Harper, 1993.
Weisbord, Marvin. *Productive Workplaces,* San Francisco: Jossey-Bass, 1987.
Gainsharing
Graham-Moore, Brian and Ross, Timothy L. *Gainsharing,* Washington, D.C.: Bureau of National Affairs, 1990.

Creating Change

Bennis, Warren G., Benne, Kenneth D.,and Chin, Robert. *The Planning of Change,* Fort Worth: Holt, Rinehart and Winston Inc., 1976.

London, Manuel. *Change Agents,* San Francisco: Jossey-Bass, 1990.

Adult Learning

Daloz, Laurent A. *Effective Teaching and Mentoring,* San Francisco: Jossey-Bass, 1987.

Shor, Ira. *Empowering Education,* Chicago: University of Chicago, 1992.

Democracy at Work

Adams, Frank T. and Hansen, Gary. *Putting Democracy to Work,* Eugene, Ore.: Hulogos' Communications, 1987.

Whyte, William Foote and Whyte, Kathleen King. *Making Mondragon* Cornell: ILR Press, 1987.

Team Building

Dyer, William G. *Teambuilding,* Reading, Mass.: Addison-Wesley, 1987.

Scholtes, Peter. *The Team Handbook,* Madison, Wis.: Joiner Associates, 1988.

Quality

Ishikawa, Kaoru. *Guide to Quality Control,* Tokyo: Asian Productivity Organization, 1974.

Personal Growth

Covey, Stephen R. *The 7 Habits of Highly Effective People,* New York: Simon and Schuster, 1989.

Guillory, William. *Realizations: Personal Empowerment Through Self-Awareness,* Salt Lake City, Utah: Innovations Publishing, 1990.

Problem Solving

Kepner, Charles and Tregoe, Benjamin. *The New Rational Manager,* Princeton, N.J.: Princeton Research Press, 1984.

As you can see, the Resource Center does not have to take up more than a couple of shelves on a bookcase somewhere in the organization. The availability of this type of information can have a significant impact on people in the organization as they awaken to the possibilities of reshaping their work environment into a more competitive and personally fulfilling setting.

DESIGNING A CONTINUOUS EDUCATION PROCESS

Although organizations exist to accomplish a wide variety of missions, one common denominator of all organizations is that they run on the same fuel, knowledge. Successful organizations function as open systems, recruiting knowledgeable people and investing in continuing education. Stagnant organizations are closed systems, keeping new knowledge out and denying information that challenges comfortable norms.

It is vital to the health of an organization to establish a process for continuous education that applies the principles of participatory action research. An organization that is pursuing the pathway of empowerment should establish an education council to assess learning needs. Like the empowerment planning team, an education council (EC) will involve people who represent the various groups within the organization. In a factory, the EC will include middle managers, facilitators, and employees from work teams with knowledge of each craft or skill area, along with a staff person who can help carry out the EC's plans.

The education council assesses the learning needs of the organization at all levels based either on their personal knowledge or by surveying the organization. Working within the organization's budget constraints, the EC must prioritize the learning needs and decide how the needs will be met.

Endulling organizations lack a participatory approach to learning. In an endulling organization, the training function is either delegated to a staff organization or used by line management in a haphazard and ineffective manner. Endulling organizations often believe they have continuing education sending one person to a seminar, but not providing for new knowledge to be shared back into the whole organization.

A continuous education process (Figure 4.6) engages the organization's education council in an on-going process of assessment, planning, learning, and application of knowledge and skills.

It is important for the EC to recognize that this is a continuous, ongoing process—not a one-time event. The assessment process can be annual

Figure 4.6
The Continuous Education Process

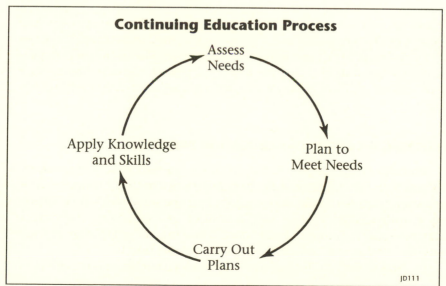

or quarterly, or on any time cycle that is natural to the system, such as prior to the beginning of the organization's fiscal year.

The EC can make important decisions on standardizing some curriculum for the overall good of the organization. For example, the EC can decide which personality profile option will be standard for the organization. The EC can render make/buy decisions for internal design or external purchase of training.

APPENDIX:
Opportunities for Praxis

1. What strengths does your organization already have in educating people regarding vocational, business, process, interpersonal, and political skills?

2. What weaknesses exist in your organization in the skill areas?

3. What steps can your empowerment planning team take to create an empowering budget cycle?

4. How are the quality tools actually *used* in your organization?

5. Which parts of your organization currently have the most empowering and democratic practices in use? How can you offer them as a model to overcome the places where your organization might be experiencing reification?

6. Can you establish a resource center? What resources will you put in your center?

5

Changing the Support Systems

> What industry has discovered is equally applicable to every
> other institution—namely, that adult education processes are
> basic tools of organizational growth and development.
> —Malcolm Knowles, *The Modern Practice of Adult Education*

Any organizational system relies on formal and informal methods to establish expectations, reward conformance to group norms, and address behavior that deviates from the organizational norms. In almost any setting, the change agent's initial efforts should focus on educating managers and employees to enable them to function in an empowering manner. This is the organizational equivalent to preparing the soil and planting the seeds of change.

As the education proceeds and peoples' behaviors start to change, the change agent must address the issues of watering, weeding, and otherwise nurturing the new growth. This brings us to the subject of changing the management support systems within an organization.

Seven Step Path to Empowerment
1. Create champions.
2. Involve people in planning the change.
3. Create team leaders.
4. Educate the workforce.
➤ 5. *Change the support system.*
6. Practice consensus decision making.
7. Involve people in strategic and tactical planning.

There is little to be gained in attempting to modify the support systems until the consciousness-raising process creates a perception within the organization that the current systems for reinforcement are rewarding the wrong behaviors. As people accept the roles and behaviors of empowerment, then new, democratic support processes will be needed.

Some will argue that the change process cannot really begin until the reinforcing systems are realigned to reinforce empowering behaviors. This is putting the cart before the horse. The people who care and feed the existing support systems, or others who rely on the system to support their current behaviors, will resist change while there is no widely held perception that democratic change is needed or desirable.

As the emancipatory education process initiates a climate of empowerment and creates a desire for change, the empowerment champions and the empowerment planning team, along with the managers of the support systems, need to modify the systems. Specific areas to address include

1. The compensation system;
2. The recognition system;
3. Performance appraisals;
4. Complaint review processes;
5. The employment and promotion process;
6. Discipline and organizational boundaries;
7. The audit function; and
8. Performance indicators.

CHANGE WITHIN AN EMPOWERING ORGANIZATION

It will be very tempting for well-meaning line and staff managers to want to use their expertise to redesign the support systems for the whole organization. The knowledge of these managers is indeed an important part of the formula for change. However, in an empowering environment, the change process needs to be based on the action research cycle. The people who work within the organization need to be involved in researching, selecting, designing, and implementing the changes to the support systems.

The staff "experts" should help facilitate the process, help identify sources for research, and provide knowledge related to the pros and cons of administering the alternatives being considered.

The empowerment planning team will build commitment to the new support systems by giving ownership of the design process to the whole organization, not just the staff specialists. It is the EPT's role to prioritize the systems that need to be changed and to charter teams to conduct the action research on each system. It is highly unlikely that an organization can overhaul more than two or three systems simultaneously-so prioritization is necessary. Changes in one support system may strengthen or weaken other systems, so again, it is prudent to move with some caution, prioritizing which systems to address first.

Prioritization should be based on need and political feasibility. Need is defined by how much impact a support system has on reinforcing empowering behaviors and the extent to which the existing system fails to reinforce empowerment and instead reinforces autocracy and endullment. Political feasibility deals with the amount of resistance the EPT is apt to encounter in redesigning the system.

Each redesign team chartered by the EPT should balance the input of the political groups within the organization. In a hospital, include representatives from nurses, physicians, technicians, and administrators. In a business, involve people whose experiences and perspectives come from all parts of the organization-not just the front office. At a college, involve the faculty, administrators, and other nonadministrative staff groups to encompass the views of every group that really makes the campus function.

FACILITATING ACTION RESEARCH

Action research engages people who work in an organization in studying the needs of their organization, identifying opportunities for change, and making decisions as to what changes should be made. People involved in action research identify needs, decide on the actions to take, implement the changes they have decided on, and then evaluate the results of those changes, making further modifications until they feel that the system is performing at an optimum level and in a manner that is favorable to the customers and the people performing the work.

When an action research team is chartered to redesign a support system, there are several steps they will need to accomplish. In most cases the team will need to

1. Define the objectives they want to achieve.
2. Research the situation.
3. Design a new system.
4. Test the new design against the objectives.
5. Plan how to implement the new design.
6. Implement and evaluate, then fine-tune.

The first step is to clearly define the objectives that the action research team wants to achieve by redesigning a support system. Objectives should focus on the end result, such as maximizing employee participation, maximizing organizational effectiveness, minimizing customer dissatisfaction, or minimizing administrative costs.

Once the team is clear on the objectives they want to achieve through a redesign process, they should conduct research into the alternatives that are available. This can be done by benchmarking other organizations, by attending conferences, by reading books, or by reviewing the current literature. Through research, the team will identify possible models or parts of a model that might work in their own organizational context.

As the team pulls together information from a variety of sources, the new ideas need to be consolidated or assembled into a design that fits the organization. The goal is not to transplant some other organization's successful model, but to bring in ideas and implement them in a manner that fits the specific needs of the team's organization.

As the team develops its model, the team should test the model against the objectives. How well will the model meet the needs that were defined in the beginning of the process? The team's goal is to find the best approach to meeting the objectives that were defined for the re-designed system. If ideas do not meet the objectives, then toss them aside and keep looking. There is little to be gained by implementing concepts that do not help achieve the organization's objectives.

When the team has distilled its research into a workable model, an implementation plan must then be developed. The team should use flow diagrams (Figure 5.1) and Gantt charts (Figure 5.2) to define the steps in changing the support system.

As the organization implements the new system, the action research team will study the implementation, evaluate the effectiveness of the new system, and make modifications as it sees fit.

THE COMPENSATION SYSTEM

An organization's current compensation system was designed to achieve specific objectives. In many cases, the system was designed so long ago that people may have forgotten what those objectives were, but nevertheless, there were objectives that drove the design of most organization's compensation systems.

Most compensation systems have been designed to reward individual performance. The system is often based on an assumption that a higher manager will be able to determine which individuals contributions merit the greatest reward. In some cases this may indeed be true. Often, these systems lead to a lack of teamwork and a lack of commitment to the organization on the part of individuals because the compensation system is perceived as being unfair.

There is no such thing as a perfect compensation system. Instead, there are systems that perform well or poorly based on the objectives that the organization is seeking to achieve. When the objective is to reinforce empowerment, there are definitely systems that perform well and many that perform poorly.

The most basic advice regarding compensation is a Biblical admonition that has been around for over 3000 years. "Muzzle not the ox that treads out the corn." The ox was the key to the agricultural system in ancient times. To muzzle the ox would save corn in the short run, but would cause the entire system to collapse in the long run. A basic objective for any compensation system should be in line with this Biblical truth-design the system so that the organization will survive in the long run.

Beyond that basic advice, the action research team will need to struggle with the objectives that their compensation system needs to achieve. The objectives will vary from one organization to the next because the business specific issues and the regional situation will differ all across the globe. There is no one system that works well in all circumstances. The action research team must find the system that fits the organization's needs and situation so that all the employees can support the compensation system as reasonable and just, even if they do not make as much money as they would like.

There are many objectives that an organization might want to support through compensation. Performance of the individual and performance of the organization might be two key objectives, but many compensation systems are tied to neither of these objectives. Some systems focus on retaining people with the greatest knowledge of the organization. Some systems focus on being able to recruit the best graduates from schools, whereas others focus on providing internal equity between different skill areas.

Many companies that have won the Malcolm Baldrige National Quality Award tie a large percentage of the employee's annual pay into a bonus based on the company's overall performance, giving these companies a motivational advantage over companies that pay salaries or wages that are not linked to organizational performance. Some organizations stay away

Figure 5.1
Flow Diagram

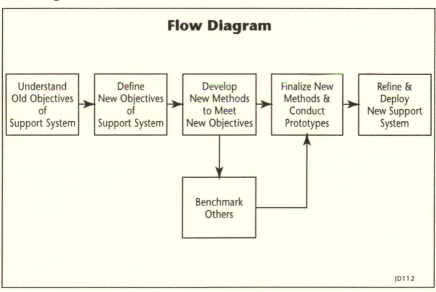

from bonus systems because they cannot agree internally on an equitable approach to distributing bonuses.

Some organizations pay more attention to the pay in their regions than they do to the performance of their organizations. The compensation specialists seem to think their job is to pay people what the prevailing local wage may be, regardless of whether or not they are making money for the organization. For a gardener, this is like saying I will only water my garden twice a week because all the other gardeners only water their gardens twice a week. I would not want to risk having a bumper crop by applying more water! What is the objective?

When organizations use area wages to set their own wages they may intend to send a message that says "Come work here, we pay as well as anyone else around here." They may also be sending a message that says "No matter how well you perform and no matter how much money you make for the organization, we will not pay you any more than the people working at the company down the highway from us that might be going out of business." Again, what is the objective that the organization seeks to achieve?

In the government sector, there are additional challenges to designing a compensation system that supports empowerment. When private sector organizations utilize teams to enhance productivity, they can reward people for team efforts because they generate profits that can be shared with the employees. When government sector employees work in teams, they find ways to save money and improve service to their customers, the

Figure 5.2
Gantt Chart

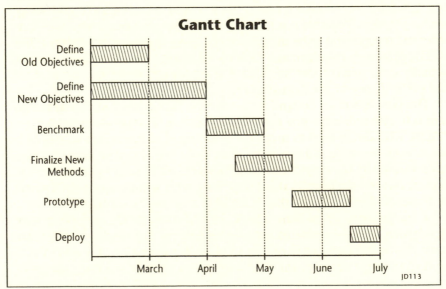

tax payers. However, government employees will not generate profits. Instead, their efforts usually lead to a reduction in taxes, so there is no fund for rewarding people for team effort. Action research teams in the government sector will need to explore nonmonitary awards that can be given, such as extra time off for community service, or sabbaticals for personal enrichment.

RECOGNITION SYSTEMS

The empowerment planning team may need to charter an action research team to study the organization's recognitions systems to assure that a credible and realistic program has been designed and implemented that encourages empowerment.

One of the interesting aspects of consulting is to visit companies and businesses and to observe their recognition systems. Have you ever gone into a fast food store and while waiting for your order, glanced around at the plaques and posters. Look for the "employee of the month" plaque that these businesses invariably display. Check it out to see if it is up to date. It is interesting to note the number of these recognition plaques that are running three to six months behind. Is it because there was no one worthy of recognition? Is it because the store manager is too busy to bother with recognition? Or is it due to the design of the recognition process that makes it unwieldy to use and of so little value to the employees that they do not question when it lapses out of date?

Recognition systems lack credibility with the employees when the authority for establishing awards and deciding who the award recipients will be resides only within management. When this is the case, employees rightfully feel endulled, and so they discount the value of the recognition program. Whether it is true or not, the endulled employees will consider the recognition to be misguided or rigged so that only a favored few will be picked by management. In these situations, a recognition program actually does much more harm than good for employee morale and for the performance of the organization.

The core lesson in designing an effective recognition and awards system is to remember the one fundamental lesson of organizational design: "Those who create tend to support." If an organization wants its employees to value its recognition system, then the system must be designed and administered by the employees. A staff person can certainly administer the details, but the decision making regarding who will be recognized must be conducted in a manner that is credible with the workforce.

A recognition design team should be chartered by the empowerment champions or the empowerment planning team. The recognition design team should be chartered to review all existing recognition and reward systems in the organization, and to change those systems to maximize credibility of the program, make administration of the program as simple as possible, and ensure that the system reinforces empowerment.

An effective recognition design team will have members that represent a variety of perspectives. There must definitely be someone who can articulate management's interests in having a recognition program. A human resources professional can add a lot to the team, but should probably not chair the team. The rest of the team should be made up of people who represent the various parts of the organization. If the organization has bargaining units that represent some of the employees, then the bargaining unit leadership should be asked to participate or designate someone to be a team member to represent their interests.

This team should start by clearly defining the objectives of having a recognition program for the organization. The objectives can be very different from one enterprise to the next. A school may have one set of objectives, whereas a retail business can have a different set of objectives. Even within a business, such as a manufacturing company, the objectives can change from one location to another. One factory might want to recognize people who have made significant cost savings contributions. Another may want to place emphasis on resolving customers' complaints. There is no one "right way" to recognize people. Each recognition system must be specific to the local need, based on the local input.

Once the objectives for the recognition system are defined, the design team can start generating options. The team can conduct a brainstorming session to invent ideas. The team can benchmark an organization that has the reputation for being the best in their field to learn how they conduct their recognition program. Or, people can get on the phone and call their contacts in other similar businesses, agencies, or schools and collect ideas.

Once the recognition design team has generated a suitable list of options, the team members need to select the options that best meet the needs of their organization. The best choices will be the options that meet the organization's needs, and can be implemented in a manner that maximizes credibility with the workforce.

Example

A chemical manufacturing plant wanted to provide recognition to employees for good teamwork. In the past, human resources would have been responsible for creating and implementing some form of new reward. In the interest of empowerment, a joint union and management team studied the need and options for providing recognition for team effort. They decided on a Team of the Month Award. A committee that would include union and salaried employees was chartered to implement the idea. The committee wrote a list of criteria for giving Team of the Month Awards, and established an award ceremony involving the plant manager. The committee now meets every month to review work groups that have been nominated and to decide which work group, if any, deserves to receive this recognition. Photographs of the Team of the Month are placed in the company's newsletter.

APPRAISAL SYSTEMS

Dr. W. Edwards Deming stirred up a great deal of controversy, often conveniently ignored by human resources professionals, regarding the negative results of most performance appraisal systems. Deming believed that the results were usually so bad that organizations would be better served to have no appraisal system at all.

Deming argued that performance appraisal systems demotivate people by placing the evaluation process into a normal distribution where most people will be considered to be performing at a common level and a few will perform well above or below the norm. Although this may be true regarding the height and weight of an organization's employees, there is no evidence to support the use of a normal distribution to describe the performance of people.

Deming also noted that many appraisal systems start by establishing goals or quotas for employee performance. In most cases, he found that this inhibits people from achieving the higher level of performance that is possible when people are allowed to work creatively, free from fear.

Many organizations design their performance appraisal from a perspective that Stephen Covey might call a scarcity mentality. High praise for people's performance is something that the organization treats as scarce, therefore quotas are imposed on the number of high ratings people can receive.

The scarcity mentality of most performance appraisal systems generally makes little sense from the perspective of how systems work. In a garden, for instance, when the gardener buys seeds, he or she does not look for the average seeds. The prize watermelon is the seed melon so that next year's crop will be even better than this year's one. All of the organization's people should be the best the organization can possibly find.

For example, several years ago I was assisting in a total quality effort at a prestigious national laboratory. All of the researchers at this facility are men and women of great genius who are an amazing resource to our country. Yet the organization insisted on evaluating these people on a normal distribution. Yes, they were all of exceptional talent, but we felt we had to distinguish between those who were of average brilliance and those of exceptional brilliance. Just imagine how that went over with an organization of supertalented people!

So, we find ourselves in a situation where Deming pointed out that the annual performance appraisal business is a no-win situation, yet most organizations still conduct them. Was Deming wrong? Probably not!

What continues to drive the performance appraisal process in most organizations is the law. Organizations need to be able to assure themselves that employees have been evaluated to protect the company (or city, or school system, or government agency) in the event of a law suit related to promotions, dismissals, or any other action.

Therefore, it is necessary for the prudent organization to devise a system that meets the legal needs of the organization, avoids the pitfalls identified by Deming, and actually does some good in the process.

It is prudent to start this discussion by examining what we know about people and what we know about feedback, largely from the field of education. Then we will examine performance feedback from a control paradigm and from an empowering paradigm.

What We Know about People

The most important thing we know about people is that they are all different. There are many models that are widely used to help understand the ways in which people differ from one another.

We recognize that people are fundamentally different in regards to the manner in which they collect and process information. There is considerable evidence that people think in different ways that are related to the dominance of their cerebral lobes. Left-brain-dominant people tend to be linear in their thinking, with a strength in mathematical thinking an logical problem solving. Right-brain-dominant people tend to collect and process information in relation to large patterns, and prefer to solve problems through creativity. Assessment instruments exist that allow individuals to understand their tendencies in using their brains. Do you want to have an appraisal system that rewards only one type of thinking process?

We also recognize a variety of traits that define the personality of an individual (see Chapter 3). A work group can easily be made up on some combinations of introverts and extroverts. Some people are more focused on maintaining amiable interpersonal relations, whereas others are thought to drive toward achieving results. Some are quick in making decisions, whereas others want to gather as much information as possible. Do you want to have an appraisal system that rewards only one type of personality in your organization?

Educators know that people have different styles of learning. Some people can learn from an abstract discussion that creates an opportunity for discovery. Others learn by touching and personally taking something apart and putting it back together. Some people learn by reading, whereas others prefer to learn by listening. Some are adept at reading diagrams and drawings, whereas others can hardly cope with a flow diagram. These differences are real and well documented. Do you want to have an appraisal system that rewards only people who are strong in one particular style of learning?

Another obvious difference among people is their physical attributes. Some are big, whereas others are small. Some are thin whereas others are heavy. Some are athletic in their free time while others are sedate. Do you want to have an appraisal system that rewards just people with a particular physical trait?

Each individual is a unique package of emotional strengths and weaknesses. Each has a unique set of formative experiences and significant emotional events in their lives. Some think that they are okay and that you are okay, too. Others think they are okay and that there is definitely something wrong with you. Each person copes with different emotional issues throughout their lives. Do you want to have an appraisal system that rewards only people whose emotional state is at a certain place?

In the field of adult development, it is widely held that each person passes through certain developmental stages in their life cycle. At each stage, people tend to have to deal with a set of issues in their lives. Some work groups have people in their early adult years mixed with people who are close to retirement. Each age cohort has different needs. Do you want to have an appraisal system that rewards only people at one stage in the adult life cycle?

People are motivated by very different things in their lives, often related to where they live. People in the urban centers on the East and West coasts seem to be highly motivated by wealth and status. People in the rural South are often more interested in having time to go hunting than in putting in extra hours to earn overtime. A diversity trainer from the East Coast was astonished in a workshop in the mid-South to find that almost everyone in her class placed a higher value on personal salvation than career success. She was used to working in a secular business environment, and suddenly found herself in the "Bible belt." Do we want to have an appraisal system that focuses on rewards that may not even motivate people?

Some will argue that an appraisal system should reward people only on the results of the work they are doing. They would say that none of the above mentioned issues, such as region, life cycle, personality traits, thinking patterns, physical attributes, and emotional attributes should enter into the equation. However, anyone who has worked around organizations knows that some people are in assignments where the opportunities to make significant contributions are greater than in other positions. Some employees are assigned to jobs that will never offer an opportunity to excel, while others have significant opportunities that allow even mediocre performance to appear wonderful.

What We Know about Feedback

The Bad News: Many people are "walking wounded" based on their experience with grades in schools. Grading from A to F has been traumatic for many people, damaging their self-esteem and creating self-fulfilled prophecies of low achievement. It is well known that many adults still panic when asked to take a test due to the trauma inflicted on them in the school system.

The Good News: When people are receptive to feedback, that is, when they see it as in their interest, feedback can be a powerful tool for improvement. Biofeedback, for instance, gives people feedback that can improve their health. In sports, frequent feedback is used to improve the performance of a team. The game film is reviewed and improvements are made. Computer games that teach skills, such as typing, provide many forms of feedback to help a person improve. Feedback is most helpful when people want to know what their current "best" is and then learn how to beat it. Feedback can be beneficial when recipients trust the person that provides the feedback and believe that the system is not rigged against them.

The Control Paradigm

Most organization's feedback systems are based on a control paradigm. Why do organizations measure performance? To reward good performers, to improve or remove poor performers, and to have a dependable system. In the control paradigm, feedback is something we do to people, not with them. We give feedback to cover the organization from legal action and to pick our best and worst performers so we can "pay for performance." So, what's wrong with that?

1. The host of differences between individuals cited above makes all systems suspect.
2. The opportunity to perform is often set by the job assignment. Some people have better assignments that give them a greater opportunity for success and advancement.
3. People are part of a work system and often cannot control the variations in the system.
4. People do not like to be manipulated unless they are the lucky few who are making the A's.
5. Over time, most people, either in schools or the workplace, want to give out As to more and more people, because the recognize the contributions of the broader group. However, this dilutes the prejudicial value of an A.

An Empowering Paradigm

From the perspective of an empowering paradigm, we ask the same question as to why we measure. We measure to enable learning, to enable growth, and because we care about each other and ourselves.

Measuring enables learning when a significant part of the process is conducted with instruments that encourage self-discovery and the creation of a personal development plan. Measurement enables growth when it helps people understand the best path they need to take in their lives and how to be at their happiest and most productive in their current work. Because we care, we want to be honest with ourselves and with each other.

With an empowering paradigm, we will encourage work groups to have performance indicators. We will encourage individuals to establish long-term and short-term goals for self-improvement and to share those quarterly with their fellow team members. We will encourage people in work groups to give each other honest peer feedback.

A System Based on Dialogue

In any organization, there is a real need for the leaders to listen to their employee's ideas about how their performance and the performance of their work group can be improved. There is also a need for the leadership to give individuals and groups feedback regarding their performance. There is a need for employees to talk to each other about performance within their team, and there is a need for leaders to receive feedback from the people they are trying to lead. Because of the duel objectives of listening and giving feedback, the term *performance dialogue* should be employed instead of performance appraisal.

We all really need honest feedback about how well we are performing in our work. This feedback may be based on many things, such as how each person relates behaviorally to other people in the workplace; how each person performs, in terms of quantity and quality of work; or how each person participates in the process of planning and achieving goals.

When leaders deny people accurate ongoing performance feedback, they are denying people the water of life. Without feedback, people are stunted in their growth. Without feedback, people may assume that their work is great, even if it is not. However, if the only time a person receives feedback is when there is a problem, people will fear their management and associate feedback with punishment.

Likewise, if leaders fail to create an opportunity to listen to their people about how the work system can be improved, then many opportunities for improvement will be missed. People may feel that their ideas are not wanted by management. In today's competitive market, this would be a terrible condition for any organization.

While recognizing the need for performance dialogue, there is also a legitimate concern regarding the individual's role as part of a work system. Opportunities for excellent performance, and cooperation from other employees, may depend on variables outside the individual's control.

Excellent performance for the overall organization will depend on cooperative efforts of many individuals. This realization has led some to note that performance feedback that isolates the individual's performance from the context of the work group creates destructive competition within organizations and generates cynicism among employees who are receiving performance feedback. To be constructive for the the organization and to the individuals, performance dialogue should

1. Be focused on the degree to which the person is contributing to the goals and objectives of the work group;
2. Be frequent and direct;
3. Be experienced as a true discussion where performance is considered from the context of the overall work group; and
4. Be designed to reinforce good performance or to help in making changes with the individual and the overall work group or the work system.

When people are working together in a work group where they share common objectives and depend on each other to achieve their objectives, people need feedback that is directed to both the group as a whole and to individual members. Feedback to the group as a whole may be verbal, such as "Everybody in the group did a good job on the project." Feedback to the group may be nonverbal, such as treating everyone to a pizza or giving everyone an incentive bonus. Dialogue for improvement should also occur at a group level in the form of a meeting. The leader must frequently find times to ask the whole group for ideas for improving performance, improving safety, providing better satisfaction for customers, for cost savings, or for the identification of problems and concerns.

On the individual level, people need an opportunity to speak with their management in private about their performance. The objective for leaders is not to pass judgment on employees, but to help people perform their jobs within the work system. This system is made up of the materials, procedures, processes, other people, and the environment in which an individual works. The supervisors must resolve problems that the system creates that interfere with people's ability to get the job done. In most cases, people need an opportunity to talk about how the system impacts their ability to perform. In a few cases, leaders need to advise individuals about improvements that are needed on the individual's part to fulfill the expectations of fellow team members and the organization as a whole.

In discussing performance from the context of the work group, leaders should focus on these areas:

1. How did the person contribute to setting and meeting the objectives of the work group?
2. Did the person make additional contributions that were outside of the work group's objectives?

3. Has the person contributed ideas for improving the system
   and/or helped to implement ideas for improvement.
4. What are the person's developmental needs and accomplishments?
5. What kind of behavior did this person use to help the work group
   achieve its objectives?

In describing a person's contributions to the overall objectives of the organization, it is best to avoid value-laden words, such as "outstanding," "acceptable," or "poor." These words may cause a person to overlook the need for cooperation from others in achieving group objectives, or may create anger at being unfavorably labeled. Overall evaluation of an individual's performance should describe how the person works in relation to the rest of the work group and in terms of individual contributions.

Figure 5.3 illustrates four quadrants of work performance, based on the measurement of individual contributions and team collaboration.

It is important for people to receive feedback that lets them know if they are participating well as a team player, or working as an individual contributor. In some lines of work, being an individual contributor is a fine thing. In other lines of work, it can be a problem.

There is no "bulletproof" method to meet the legal need for documented feedback while avoiding the pitfalls that Dr. Deming has identified. However, using a design that encourages dialogue and that avoids descriptive titles, such as "excellent" can provide a method for effective communication within an organization.

Figure 5.3
Quadrants of Work Performance

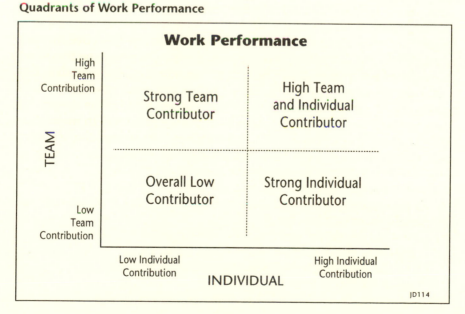

Some organizations are experimenting with 360 degree performance appraisals in which each employee receives feedback from peers as well as managers. Managers receive feedback from the people they lead, from fellow managers, and from the people to whom they report.

As with the compensation system and the recognition system, an action research team will need to be formed to design the organization's performance appraisal system. Again, the human resources organization has experts that can help, but it is important for the ownership of the system to be with the people in the organization, not with the staff experts.

There are a great many new ideas being circulated about the redesign of performance appraisals. Take the time to identify the objectives your organization wants to achieve, and the check out some options. Ask your nearest library to run a literature search to get some up-to-date articles, or attend a conference on new systems. Generate several alternatives, and then see which one can best be tailored to meet your specific needs.

COMPLAINT REVIEW SYSTEMS

One of the fundamental features of any democratic system, whether the system is as large as a nation or as small as a local business, is the presence of a formal, equitable process for resolving individual's complaints.

When the members of an organization have a concern, they will normally want to take that issue up with the formal leadership of the organization. This might mean talking to the team's leader-facilitator, or to an ombudsman who is designated the responsibility for dealing with complaints. There are times when an organization can benefit from having an established system for providing peer review of individual's concerns.

As organizations encourage employee involvement, the issue of fair complaint resolution becomes a critical pinch point. If the organization clings to a control-oriented resolution system, employees will doubt the sincerity of the empowerment message. At some time, the empowerment planning team will need to charter an action research team to develop a new, more democratic, complaint review system.

As in other systems improvements, the team will want to establish objectives such as maximizing credibility with employees, enhancing management confidence in using a complaint system, and the encouragement of ethical conduct in the organization. With clarity of objectives, the action research team can benchmark and review literature to develop alternatives. Then the team needs to settle on their best redesign and work on implementing it.

Example

One factory chose to establish a complaint review board for reviewing all employee complaints. When an employee has a complaint that cannot be resolved with management, the employee takes the issue to a human resources staff person. The staff professional seeks to resolve the complaint, working as an ombudsman on the employee's behalf. If the human resources staff cannot resolve the issue to the employee's satisfaction, a complaint review board will be convened.

A board is established for each complaint from a pool of fifty potential board members. These fifty people were nominated by an employee council that represented all employee groups in the factory. The list of board nominees was reviewed and approved by the factory's management. If management had questioned the appropriateness of any nominee, the employee council would agree to remove that nominee from the pool of board members. (To date, management has never found any nominees to be unsuitable.) This check and balance system assures that all complaint review board members are credible to management and the workforce.

For each complaint, a board of six people is selected from the pool. The employee with the complaint may select three of the people to serve on the board. The human resources manager selects the other three. Management agrees to abide by the decision of the complaint review board.

In a unionized environment, the union is supposed to serve as the voice of the employee through a grievance process. Unfortunately, many grievance procedures encourage negotiation over positions instead of seeking answers. Labor relations professionals on management's side often feel pressured to "win" and support management instead of seeking answers that are fair or in the the best interest of the organization. In some cases, union leaders are forced to represent an employee in a grievance, even when they doubt the validity of the grievant's position, out of fear of being sued by an employee for failure to provide representation.

In some cases, union and management representatives will trade wins and losses on grievances, using the employees' problems as bargaining chips.

When labor and management can agree on the value of empowerment and democracy, they can work together to design win-win systems to resolve employee and management concerns. In the absence of a shared value on both sides regarding democratic processes, labor and management will have great difficulty in designing a system that provides win-win results.

An action research team would be needed to develop the specific model of a review board that works for an organization. Of special concern in the design process is the need to identify the boundaries for what issues can and cannot be brought before a review board. For instance, an organization may designate special problems, such as sexual harassment or racial discrimination, as outside the boundaries of a review board and more appropriate for investigation by professional human resources staff and line management. Complaints about individuals might likewise be outside the boundaries of a review board and better directed to discussion with line management. However, if an employee is unhappy about not being selected for a job, or disappointed with a performance review, a review board might provide a fair and open way for that person to have the organization's actions reviewed.

THE EMPLOYMENT AND PROMOTIONAL PROCESS

Of all the activities in which organizations engage, there are few that are more critical than the decisions regarding who to entrust as members and who to develop as leaders.

In an autocratic and control-oriented culture, the selection process is controlled by managers who may use the process as a reward system and to secure and enlarge their hold over their organizational fiefdom. New people may be expected to give allegiance to their manager as a veritable liege lord.

The promotional process in an autocratic system may likewise meet combined objectives, such as reward for loyalty and obedience and as a process to ensure the continuance of a control oriented culture.

Empowerment leads to the expectation among the workforce that within reasonable boundaries, the selection process will become participative and the leadership process will evolve to become consistent with democratic principles.

The empowerment planning team will need to charter an action research team to re-design the employment and promotional process so that they will eventually support a democratic culture within the organization.

There are many good examples in the current literature of highly participative employment processes that reinforce a philosophy of empowerment. The action research team will need to review the literature and conduct some benchmarking to develop an alternative suitable to the specific needs of the organization.

Example

A college decided to implement a more democratic process for hiring new professors. In the past, the decisions were made by the academic dean. The college initiated a new process whereby applicants would be interviewed by a committee consisting of other faculty and honor students. The faculty supported this system since it allowed them to recruit compatible peers whose areas of expertise would best round out the academic team. Student leaders believed that their involvement in the selection process helped ensure that new faculty could communicate effectively with students. The academic dean's interests were protected by initial screening of the applicants prior to the interviews.

Example

The manager of a 450-person organization was selecting a new senior manager who would manage one third of the organization. In the past, the manager would interview and select the new member of his management staff. Under a new empowerment initiative, the manager formed a team that included the other senior managers and employees from the part of the organization that the new manager would lead. The selection team defined the criteria for a successful candidate, helped identify possible candidates for the position, and made a recommendation of their top choices. The manager confirmed their top choice and promoted that person to the senior management position.

In most cases, the employment process of an organization involves a variety of decisions that must be reached in series. These decisions can be made in many ways as long as the organization is cognizant of what the approved process may be.

The first issue in an employment process is designating who has the authority and responsibility to decide that an open position exists that can be filled. In many organizations, this decision requires the agreement of the financial organization, which must verify that funds exist to pay for a new person. There must be a check and balance process built into any organization's process to ensure that the decision to hire is based on available funding.

In some cases, the best option is not to hire, but to subcontract a service. Subcontracting can work, when there is a clear division of tasks or a clear geographical boundary that separates people who are part of the organization from those who are providing a specific service. However, organizations need to be extremely aware of the impact of using "temporary" workers as opposed to hiring full-time, full-fledged members of the organization. Using temporary people might be an effective way to screen potential new hires, but temporary people cannot be expected to be satisfied with a status that disfranchises them from participation in the decision making of a work process. If great care is not taken, the contracted staff soon begin to feel like servants, and the regular organization members can start to act like aristocrats.

When an organization has decided to fill a position, the next question is how. A professional staff can be used to handle the process, and managers can be used to interview and make hiring decisions. However, an action research team can find many ways to make the process more participative, thereby improving the results of the hiring process.

First of all, the action research team can examine the process for deciding whether or not a position can be filled. Having an employee representative participate in this early part of the decision making process can help ensure that employees' perspectives are being taken into account. Whereas a manager may desire to fill a position, an employee may see a way that the work can be reassigned. Sometimes, the motivation for filling positions is to increase the size of a manager's domain, instead of accomplishing a work objective.

Next, the action research team can review the process for screening applicants. The process can be redesigned to include a team member from the work group where an opening exists in the interviewing process. Or, the interview process can be designed where all of the team members participate in the interview process and have input into the decision along with management. The process can even be designed where management grants the decision-making authority entirely to the team.

Like any participative system, it is important to design in a check and balance system. If the employees are given full authority to conduct the interviews, the human resources organization might be given the responsibility to first screen the applicants to ensure that everyone who is interviewed meets basic educational standards or requirements for experience.

Promotional Systems

In any truly democratic system, leaders are elected. There is ample evidence to support the fact that elected leadership provides a viable and effective form of leadership in business, military, and administrative settings (see Chapter 8). Most organizations will have to wrestle with the transition from selecting leaders in an autocratic manner to a democratic selection process.

The empowerment planning team will need to develop a long-term transitionary plan for implementing democratic selection of leaders, since this one issue has a tremendous impact on the health of the whole organization and is the single most profound change that a company, school, or other organization can make.

The key to democratizing the selection process is in first opening up the opportunity for training and education that supports leadership development. In autocratic organizations, the opportunity for education that enables advancement is often limited to a select few and becomes a self-fulfilling prophecy. To democratize the leadership selection process, the pool of potential leaders must first be enriched.

When the organization has developed a broad range of potential leaders, then a democratization process can be designed and gradually implemented. Where self-managed teams already exist, the team may already be sending a delegate to attend management meetings and to represent their interests.

Where self-managed teams do not exist, new front-line supervisor positions can be filled by allowing crews or teams to elect their leaders.

The Mondragon model (Chapter 6) provides a clear example of how a fairly large organization of more that twenty thousand people function profitably by electing front-line leaders, electing middle managers from among their front line leaders, and electing senior managers from the middle management ranks.

In very large organizations, where the stock holders' interests are represented by a board of directors, there are many approaches for democratizing the leadership selection process. Employee representatives on the board may be all that is needed, in some cases.

Large organizations can implement assessment centers to identify leadership candidates. A review board, with management, employee, and stockholder representation, can be used to select leaders who will keep the interests of all these stakeholders in mind.

DISCIPLINE AND ORGANIZATIONAL BOUNDARIES

The only effective, empowering discipline is discipline agreed to and administered by the members of the organization. This can be self- discipline or peer discipline, but not discipline decided on and administered solely by the leadership.

The key to discipline is effective goal setting, reward and recognition, and performance dialogue. All of these function best when designed to reinforce empowerment as a vital organizational value. Boundaries must be established by the group and agreed to by consensus as necessary for the benefit of the entire organization.

Establishment of Boundaries

Setting appropriate boundaries for an empowered organization is a vital task akin to setting out and controlling a strawberry patch. Strawberries are set out in a defined area. In their very first season each plant will send out runners that take root in the ground around the original plant and create new strawberry plants. The establishment of the new plants is usually a desirable occurrence. However, the gardener usually does not want the runners heading out of the boundaries of the patch, so those runners must be cut. Likewise, other plants must not be allowed to grow within the boundary of the patch or they may choke out the strawberries.

Within a teamwork environment, the boundaries of the team need to be clearly defined. When working within these boundaries, the team should be left to its own wisdom for accomplishing tasks. If the team's actions start to cross the established boundaries, then the reasons need to be examined and either the boundaries should be redefined or the team's actions change to stay within the boundaries.

The exact nature of the boundaries will obviously vary from team to team. In many cases, the boundaries should define legal requirements that the team must meet, such as Occupational Safety and Health Administration or environmental laws. Usually the team needs to be given a budget and given authority to make decisions on how to spend the budget as long as the budget is not exceeded. Performance expectations for customer satisfaction might be defined as boundaries.

The establishment of boundaries provides many advantages for increased control of the workplace. Under traditional management practices, the supervisor has responsibility for controlling issues in the workplace such as budget, safety, health, and production. Employees play a game of "Mother, may I?" with ideas that are often rejected, leading to endullment. In an empowered team with established boundaries, all the team members share the responsibility for control of the workplace. Instead of one person watching out for OSHA violations, there are now many watching. Instead of one person being concerned about productivity, everyone on the team shares the concern. Since the empowered team members are more informed about the workplace, they better understand why suggestions will or will not work.

The effect of creating empowered teams is to increase the level of control in an organization, since all team members take on responsibilities for control. The key to obtaining this heightened level of control is the establishment of boundaries.

There are all sorts of issues that can be defined within a team's boundaries. Boundaries may include service or production goals, budget limits, time tables, or requirements for coverage of shifts. Empowered teams can be given the authority to spend, schedule vacation, and provide sick leave if the performance related boundaries are being honored.

Once boundaries are agreed to and established, everyone in the organization shares the responsibility of controlling the boundaries. This was expressed by the Greek leader, Xenophon, when he was elected to lead an army of 10,000 Greek soldiers out of Persia. Xenophon admonished each soldier to act as an officer would in upholding discipline. The soldiers recognized that the established boundaries must be maintained for the welfare of all.

Work teams need the authority (subject to a complaint review process) to discipline team members who cross organizational boundaries. This authority needs to extend to the responsibility to fire people who cannot meet the team's expectations. Human resources professionals can enable this process by writing guidelines for teams to follow.

Example

A large production plant of over seven thousand people maintained a photography department that had five photographers. Traditionally, this group had a supervisor that decided how to assign the photographic tasks. However, the group frequently experienced employee complaints and morale problems, even though the supervisor was regarded as a "good" supervisor. The manager of the facility decided to turn the photographers into a self-managed team. At first, the team members had concerns, since some had aspired to become the next supervisor. However, within a few months, the team had established its boundaries and took full responsibility for the decision making and control of their work. Within a year they had reduced costs, eliminated a hazardous waste stream, and been recognized as an outstanding team in the facility.

THE AUDIT FUNCTION

Any highly empowering and democratic system does run the potential risk of abuse of leadership and suboptimization of team goals over broader organizational goals. These same risks exist in autocratic organizations as well. Effective education and training of leaders can go a long way toward heading off this potential problem.

However, organizations can further safeguard their health, effectiveness, and profitability through the proper use of an audit function. The empowerment planning team may need to charter an action research team to overhaul the organization's current audit program to make it supportive of an empowering workplace.

In an age when organizations are empowering workers, building quality into products, and using statistical control limits to control quality, some might argue that the audit is no longer necessary. It is true that poorly conducted audits contribute to overcontrol in organizations, instilling fear and misleading management with inaccurate information. However, if an organization knows why it is auditing and knows how to manage the audit process, well-managed audits will provide a process to foster learning, communication, and internal improvement vital to success.

Audit Basics

Organizations have a legitimate need for an independent, unbiased assessment of activities. In spite of the best intentions, deviations from expected procedures may occur in almost any work setting. Line managers or team members may filter their problems from the next level of leadership so issues that need attention may go unresolved. Audits also provide confirmation of excellent performance that can be internally benchmarked by the rest of the organization.

W. Edwards Deming argued that over 85 percent of the problems in a workplace can be improved only by management improving the work systems. In an empowering workplace, the employees join with management to fix the systems through action research. The audit can be a positive tool for finding the opportunities for continuous improvement. The area to be audited should be defined by the leadership, based on what the leadership thinks the organization needs to know about itself. Working like a photographer, the auditor enters the work area to take "snapshots" of how work processes are being conducted to see whether actual performance matches expectations. The auditor seeks out accurate images of improvement opportunities and examples of excellence in the organization.

An audit is an expensive investment for any organization. There is the cost of the auditor, the time that those being audited spend preparing for the audit, the cost of conducting the audit itself, and the time spent for reports and meetings to discuss audit findings. To maximize the return on such an investment, the organization must carefully consider the objectives to achieve through the quality audit. The basic questions to be addressed are, what do you care about, and what do you want to know about? A general assignment that asks the auditors to roam about the organization and see if they can uncover any problems is ineffective and creates problems for the auditor and auditees alike.

A well-defined audit will ask the auditor to examine how one specific practice is being conducted across a large part of an organization. Or it will instruct the auditor to examine several specific practices in one unit of the organization. In either case, there is a clear definition of mission for the auditor.

In defining the audit's mission, the organization should place the highest emphasis on obtaining verification that the most vital work is being performed properly. What may be most vital will certainly vary from one organization to the next. In all cases, the value of the audit will be proportional to the value that the audited area has to the organization.

Communication and Expectations

The effectiveness of the audit will be greatly influenced by how management communicates the purpose and performance of the audit. Most people do not look forward to being audited and will probably dread the prospect. This can lead to conflict in the auditing process and an effort by auditees to divert the auditor from observing the real conditions of a work process. Proper communication of the audit and ethical conduct on the part of the auditors can go a long way to ensuring cooperation with the audit process.

Effective audits begin with a statement by the organization that a particular work process is extremely vital to the welfare of the organization, so vital, in fact, that the organization is willing to go to added expense to have an independent review of the work performance. The purpose of the audit must be stated as an effort to gain a clear understanding of the status of a work situation to maintain and improve the process and to identify areas of excellence in the organization. The emphasis on understanding, continuous improvement, and identifying excellence will help create an atmosphere in which it is permissible and nonthreatening to discuss quality problems with the auditor.

Where should the expectations of performance in the workplace come from? Not the auditor! When auditors set the performance expectations, the expectations will vary from auditor to auditor. Standards for expected performance should be generated and agreed to internally through a consensus process or through the adoption of standards agreed on within an industry. The boundaries established for work teams and the performance indicators used in the organization should offer guidance in establishing the standards against which an audit will be conducted.

Empowering Audits

The most important part of an audit is not what the auditor does in collecting the data, but what the leadership does with the audit information. Leaders must be prepared to initiate actions to correct deviations and to celebrate excellence. The actions taken to make improvements must not make the situation worse. The best approach is to meet with the people involved in the deviation and ask for their ideas for improving the situation and to empower them to solve the problem. This allows them to assume ownership for the problem and for the solution. Leaders must then seek commitment from people to resolve the problem within a certain time frame and make resources available to support improvements, if necessary.

The most effective resolutions of audit findings occur when the organization has systems in place that allow for employee participation and an open climate for discussions about problems and opportunities as part of the normal business environment. Joint union-management efforts for achieving quality are ideal for addressing audit concerns. Elected employee councils offer another good channel for addressing issues in a democratic manner. Creating cross-functional teams will often provide a good vehicle for making improvements that reinforce empowerment.

The audit can become a powerful tool for feeding a continuous improvement process and providing recognition for excellence in any organization. A successful audit process that reinforces empowerment requires positive expectations about how audits will be conducted, identification of important areas for auditing, positive communication to the workforce about the purpose of the audit, and involving people in following up on the audit findings.

PERFORMANCE INDICATORS

The final support system that may require adjustment to support empowering work processes is the organization's performance indicator system. For some organizations, this may need to be the first system to be redesigned by an action research team.

Have you ever imagined what it would be like to drive a car with no speedometer and no gas gauge? Do you think that driving under these conditions would increase your chances of getting ticketed or running out of gas? Perhaps to compensate you would drive slower than you need to, and would spend more time at the gas station topping off your tank.

What if you were driving a bus and there is a speedometer, but it is located at the back of the bus? The person riding in the back has to pass the word up through the rows to tell the driver when to slow down and when to speed up. How efficient that would be!

These conditions are exactly what occurs in many work settings. The people with their hands on the steering wheel, the daily contact with customers, suppliers, equipment, and reports, do not have access to the performance indicators to help them know when they are doing well and when they are in danger.

In one particular organization, a manager collected a whole notebook of indicators that could be reviewed. These indicators were almost worthless since the people doing the work never found out what the indicators said. In fact, the indicators were worse than useless because a lot of resources were being spent to collect the data that were not being shared. There was no added value to the work of data collection.

In many organizations, one of the most significant factors in turning around performance has been the open and honest display of performance data in the work areas where employees can finally find out how they are doing and what is going on in the organization.

A viable set of performance indicators will give information that reflects both the internal and external perspectives of the organization. Internal indicators might include scrap rates or defects, absenteeism, alignment of spending with budgets, and the amount of overtime being worked. External indicators deal with the level of customer complaints, on-time delivery of products, and levels of sales or services provided. Both perspectives are needed to create an informed workforce that can effectively participate in an empowered manner.

Developing a good set of performance indicators for any team or organization is like pitching a pup tent on a hilltop during a wind storm. To be effective, one must peg down both sides of the tent, meaning both internal and external measures of performance. A well-set tent will have six to eight pegs all around to hold it in place, just as a good set of indicators will consist of six to eight indicators.

When only one or two performance indicators are used to give people feedback, the indicators may skew the team's performance, driving people to excel on the indicators while other unmeasured activities suffer. Any individual can corrupt a measurement system that focuses only on one or two items. This corruption can be very bad for the overall performance of the system since it may result in the suboptimization of tasks. This problem occurs in any setting where we attempt to monitor performance. If we evaluate teachers based on students' test scores, teachers are tempted to teach to the test. If we evaluate people strongly on their attendance rate, they may show up for work when they are ill and make others sick. You get the behaviors that you measure, so it is advisable to be aware of what you are really asking for.

Dr. Deming used to ask over and over in his lectures how we could expect more from workers when they did not have the performance feedback that can be derived from the display of statistical information. "How could they know?" was Deming's refrain. The people with their hands on the wheel needed profound knowledge, according to Deming. This profound knowledge was based on factual information gathered and analyzed with the understanding of the concepts of special cause and common cause variation.

APPENDIX:
Opportunities for Praxis

1. Examine your organization's current compensation system. Does it reinforce teamwork or autocratic control of the organization?

2. Examine your organization's recognition system. Are awards and recognition bestowed based on a participative process that involves all of the stakeholders, or solely by the organization's leadership?

3. Examine your organization's performance appraisal system. How does your current system encourage dialogue and learning?

4. When an organization has a complaint in your current organization, how is it handled? Does your current system provide for a fair process to resolve employee concerns?

5. How does your organization select its future leaders? Is this topic ever even discussed? If not, why not?

6. If you were to redesign your organization's audit system, what steps would you take to create a system that fosters empowerment?

7. How does your organization currently use performance indicators?

6

Consensus Decision Making

> When you have made your employees feel that they are in
> some sense partners in the business, they do not improve the
> quality of their work, save waste in time and material, because
> of the Golden Rule, but because their interests are the same
> as yours.
> —Mary Parker Follett, *Dynamic Administration*

Mary Parker Follett, whose career spanned the adult education and business education fields in the mid-twentieth century, correctly observed that participation leads to commitment in any work setting. Whether an organization is owned by its employees, by investors, or by a governmental body, participation in decision making by the workforce engenders commitment to achieving the organization's mission, vision, and goals.

Seven Step Path to Empowerment
1. Create champions.
2. Involve people in planning the change.
3. Create team leaders.
4. Educate the workforce.
5. Change the support system.
➤ 6. *Practice consensus decision making.*
7. Involve people in strategic and tactical planning.

As an organization moves toward empowering its workforce and replacing autocratic support systems with new processes that reinforce democracy, it becomes vital for the organization's leaders and members to actively practice consensus decision making in many ways. This is not to say that 100 per cent of the decisions in an organization must be made by consensus. Rather, there needs to be a consensus as to which decisions will be delegated to individuals to be made just by individuals, and which need to be made in a participative manner. If a person is empowered to make decisions for an organization, such as purchasing lumber, writing software, scheduling classes, selling to customers, or giving medication, then that person should be free to make the decisions necessary for that position. On the other hand, the organization needs to clearly identify decisions that should be made through consensus, such as hiring people, changing policies, and establishing strategic plans.

This chapter examines the underlying reasons for involving people in decision making, the use of councils to enable consensus decision making, specific tools that support consensus decision making, and a review of the dynamics of groups that will impact the consensus decision making process.

REASONS FOR INVOLVING PEOPLE

Those who create tend to support. That is the the bottom line to establishing an effective organization. An organization where the employees take an active role in planning goals, designing the workplace, and planning how to implement needed changes will be a vibrant, healthy place to work.

It has been well known for over seventy-five years that any company can greatly enhance productivity by involving its employees in decision making. The two greatest periods of industrial efficiency in America both occurred in times when managers decided to seriously involve employees in planning. Both of these times occurred during major world wars.

The First World War saw the widespread creation of work councils that gave employees input in planning and decision making. Production soared. After the war, the nation entered into a brief recession and a struggle by management to regain the exclusive right to plan how work would be performed.

Again in a time of crisis, the Second World War repeated the productivity miracle through the creation of union-management cooperation to achieve unprecedented levels of productivity. This was again followed by a struggle in which managers sought to regain the exclusive right to plan.

By now many people know how the winning allies planted the seed for higher productivity in the defeated German and Japanese nations. The British installed the practice of labor participation in the management of German companies; a practice called codetermination. The Americans introduced work team concepts to the Japanese during the MacArthur occupation.

For two decades after the war, American managers sought to retain the exclusive right to design the workplace and make business plans. Millions of dollars were given by companies to endow universities to expand business schools that would produce the managers needed to retain exclusive control of the workplace.

Nevertheless, the issue of participation continued to remain alive. First, there were researchers in the business schools who kept bringing up the issue through studies which showed the increased production of participative workplaces. Then came the increasing threat of German and Japanese penetration of American markets with high-quality and lower-cost goods.

In their panic to meet Japanese competition, Americans began to reintroduce their own concepts of participation, which had worked so well to win the Second World War. The first fledgling effort was the quality circle movement. Quality circles played an important role in convincing many supervisors and managers that there actually was some virtue to participation, as long as it did not get out of hand. The movement failed, however, because the workers involved in quality circles soon found them to be a form of pseudo-empowerment. The quality circle resembled the high school student council in which the students occupied a subordinate role and were allowed to make only minor decisions within carefully controlled boundaries. The quality circles could spend one hour of a forty-hour week in a participative setting, and had to spend the remaining thirty-nine hours in the traditional autocratic setting.

As quality circles were introducing managers to new concepts, the United States began to gain from the insights of a process called sociotechnical redesign, advanced by the Tavistock Institute in England. In this process, workers were involved in redesigning their workplace to implement new technology and new patterns of cooperation. An offshoot from this process was the new knowledge of self-managed work teams.

At this time, there are numerous companies experimenting and using self-directed work teams. An avalanche of data is now being created by business school professors and practitioners who are sharing the positive and negative experiences with these teams.

For example, *Industry Week Magazine* now conducts a Top Ten Factories in America award program. In every one of the 1994 best factories recognized by Industry Week, employees were organized into highly participative work teams and consensus decision making was becoming more important.

THOSE WHO CREATE TEND TO SUPPORT

Not many people take the time to wash and vacuum a rental car. Many people will spend the weekend washing and waxing their own car. This is likewise true of the workplace. For most people, the workplace is a rental car in which they feel no ownership. Managers want people's commitment without offering a real stake in the enterprise.

There exists a wide spectrum of ways to involve employees in the work process. The minimum formula for success is to involve people in the design of the workplace, business planning, and a share in the profits. A maximum formula is employee ownership of the majority of the enterprise.

When people are engaged through the planning and design of the workplace, they have a stake in the outcome and will work more diligently for success. On the other hand, when people are told where to sit and what to do, they become passive and alienated from their work.

People who are engaged in their work will bring more energy to the workplace and will put extra effort into the success of the enterprise. People who are not engaged in their work will become endulled to the workplace, spending their time as idly as possible and saving their energy for their own off-the-job activities. How many supervisors would be amazed to see their lazy employees hard at work at home on projects, working off-shift on their farms or gardens, or taking leadership roles in a civic organization!

Endullment is the dulling of people's minds as a result of their non-participation in any system. It's symptoms are low motivation, burnout, poor attendance, refusal to cooperate or to improve the system, pessimism, and fatalism. Ira Shor has observed the process of endullment in the school system where students have no participation or control over the learning process. The same phenomena occurs in the workplace. The formula for turning endulled workers into active participants is rather straightforward. Bring people into the planning cycle, give them boundaries and autonomy within those boundaries, and give them a personal stake in the outcome of the work being performed.

MANY LEVELS OF INVOLVEMENT

There are many levels in which employees of an organization can be engaged in the decision-making process, as shown in Table 6.1. At a basic level, the members of a work group can be provided with information about their group's performance and can take the initiative to make decisions about how to best meet customers' expectations, lower costs, and help the organization maintain a competitive position.

In a more advanced setting, employees can be given expanded responsibility for self-supervision on a daily basis and can send representation to participate in larger group meetings. These employees can also be asked to participate in any redesign of their workplace as new equipment is designed and brought into the work environment.

There is really no doubt that organizations with high levels of employee involvement perform better than their traditional counterparts. There is fifty years worth of studies and examples to verify this conclusion. The problem is in overcoming the threat to exclusive power and position that many managers mistakenly believe is theirs to exercise in the workplace.

A systems perspective regarding the true nature of the workplace will enable managers to understand that their role is to serve the whole system and to maximize the involvement of people in the decision making process in order to maximize the success of the enterprise.

Example

An excellent illustration of the results of empowerment and consensus decision making can be seen at the steam plant at a federal research facility. The steam plant had been viewed for several decades as the least desirable place at the facility to work. Employees who were not highly regarded were sometimes sent there as punishment. The old steam plant was dirty and neglected and morale was low.

A new department manager was given responsibility for the steam plant. This manager decided there was a potential rose garden in this overgrown plot of organizational weeds, so he set about the process of change.

The manager involved the workers in the process of planning and implementing the change. Over the course of a year, the facility went from being a dirty and disorderly place to become a model facility. The employees made decisions about what needed to be done. Management's job was to come up with resources to support what the employees decided needed to happen.

One action at the steam plant was the development of a mission statement. Most people may think that the mission of a steam plant was to make steam. But the more insightful workers observed that the mission of the steam plant was to provide comfort to their clients. They wanted clients to walk into offices and laboratories and to not have to think at all

Table 6.1
Levels of Organizational Involvement

	Business	Education	Government
Major system	Entire corporation system	Major university or a large school	Major state or federal agency
Local organization	Individual factory	College or single school	Regional office
Organization units	Production line or department	Academic sections (history, math)	Local office
Team level	Work team	Classroom	Work team

as to whether it was too hot or cold. The system should be invisible and should please the customers.

With that in mind, the supervisors had to rethink their role. If the mission of the steam plant was to provide comfort to their clients, what then was the role of supervision? The supervisors discovered that the role of supervision was to get the rocks out of the road so that the workers could achieve their mission.

One of the major obstacles to the reform of the steam plant was the need for repainting. After the workers pointed out the need for repainting, management requested the allocation of a painter to the building. Of course this was initially turned down, since the facility did not traditionally allocate painters to facilities. However, management worked very diligently to get this rock out of the road and succeeded in bringing in a painter.

The story goes that the painter showed up on the first day and said, "I'm here. What do you guys want me to paint?" And the workers replied, "You don't understand how we do things around here. You're the painter, you decide what you need to paint." After he had overcome the initial shock, the painter got into the swing of things.

The painter decided what to paint and set his own schedule. He made numerous suggestions for how the painting could be speeded up and his sensible management got him what he needed. The painter even started

Table 6.2
Models for Governing Organizational Levels

Major systems	Representatives from each factory, business unit, college in a university, or regional office in a major state or federal agency participate in the top level governing body. (Mondragon model)
Local Organization	Representatives from each major group in a factory, college, high school, or regional office participate on a governing body. (Plant council or All-College council model)
Organizational Units	Representatives from each team or interest group participate on a governing body. (Division council or Whitley council model)
Team level	Involvement of 100 percent of the team in tactical and strategic planning for the team, in setting boundaries, performance indicators, and in regular team meetings that practice consensus decision making.

doing his own research on new kinds of paint which would be more resistant to the high temperatures on the surface of the furnaces that needed to be painted.

Not to be outdone, the janitor suggested waxing the floors. In the previous forty years of operation of this steam plant, nobody had ever waxed the floors. Can you imagine how the typical janitor would react to a request from management to wax the floors in a steam plant? But when the idea came from the janitor, instead of from management, it was successful because *those who create tend to support.*

The building operators told the janitor to try waxing the floors in just one area to see how it would look. It looked great, and they all said so. So, the janitor went on to wax all the floors.

In a few months, the steam plant went from a dismal place of dispair into an upbeat model of effective operation of a coal fired steam plant. People began to come in to visit the facility and marvel at its appearance and performance. A visitor's log in the supervisor's office shows people from all across the United States who have come to see the steam plant.

Of course, not all visitors understand what they see. One visitor reviewed the facility and then went back and had management develop their plan for renewing their facility in a like manner. They did not involve their employees, so their estimate for refurbishment was three times the cost of the plan developed by the employees at the steam plant.

Participation in planning and decision making energizes people in the workplace. People who are turned off by their jobs can be enlivened by having an opportunity to influence and control how they live their lives at work. Another vital area for participative decision making involves the selection of performance measures for the work group.

Not every decision in this illustration required a consensus of the whole group. The painter was empowered to make the necessary decisions as to what to paint. The consensus was the need to paint. The janitor took the individual initiative to wax a part of the floors. The group made the decision for the work to be expanded. With consensus about mission and broad objectives, individuals are empowered to take specific actions, as long as they are within understood boundaries.

MODELS FOR DIFFERENT ORGANIZATIONS

Table 6.1 showed that there are various levels or sizes of organizations that can practice empowerment and consensus decision making. Table 6.2 illustrates the models that exist for providing governance for these different levels.

THE TEAM MODEL

Many organizations are experimenting with a team model for creating an empowering workplace. The team model focuses on the work group, such as a production line, a road repair crew, the nurses in a ward, the sales staff in a store, or the fire fighters on a shift.

In the team model, the team members must cooperate and collaborate to achieve a mission that they all share. The team should be able to agree on their mission and have performance indicators that give them feedback as to how well they are meeting their mission. At a team level, people can establish a long-term vision of what they want to achieve and can develop a plan with specific goals and milestones to be reached.

People who are working in a team model need to designate a specific time for regular meetings to discuss their efforts. As a team matures, it takes on more and more of the decision making that used to belong to management, such as job assignments, vacation scheduling, control of the budget, and the other reinforcing processes discussed in Chapter 5.

New teams may need a facilitator who will work closely with the group to monitor meetings and help the group interface with the next higher level in the organization structure. In an organization with a mature team model, one facilitator may serve seven or more teams, meeting with each team once a week or every other week to help the team work through its issues.

THE DIVISION COUNCIL MODEL

In small organizations, there may not be a level higher that the team. However, in larger organizations, teams may work to provide services and functions that are part of a larger division. In this situation the division council model allows the teams to integrate their issues and activities through a council form of governance.

Division council members are sent as delegates from each of the teams. For example, if a division is the production part of a factory, each production team sends a delegate to the council. The council makes decisions that impact all the teams, such as allocation of budgets, discussion of customer concerns, and policies that impact the teams in the division, such as work scheduling. Council issues often deal with establishing the boundaries for the teams and reviewing the performance indicators for all the teams and the division as a whole.

In one organization, special attention was given to ensure that representation on a council was diverse based on the types of employees in that organization. Some were chemists and others were lab analysts, and there was a desire to ensure that both groups were represented, so that all the teams did not end up sending chemists to represent them on the council.

A division council should have a charter that defines its mission, a clear definition of its boundaries, and a definition of how members of the council are selected. The council needs to have regularly scheduled meetings with agreed upon agendas. The council needs to use consensus decision-making methods (described later in this chapter).

Councils need to rotate the responsibility for chairing the council, and should always provide minutes that make it easy for council members to communicate back with their teams. Councils may benefit from a neutral facilitator who can focus on using participative processes that will free the council members to focus on the content of the decisions and plans that must be developed.

THE PLANT MODEL (ALL-COLLEGE COUNCIL)

In larger organizations, such as a college, a hospital, a factory, or a major branch of government, an all college council model will ensure democratic participation in decision making.

The all college council model was advanced in the 1970s in educational settings to promote collaborative decision making. A council would be established that had representatives from faculty, students, administrators, alumni, and trustees. The council would meet periodically to establish the college's strategic and tactical plans. Major decisions, such as the initiation of a fund-raising program, would be brought before the council. Faculty and students representatives have an equal voice and the opportunity to bring forward issues for discussion and decision making.

This same model has been used in factories. Each division council will select two people to represent the division on the plant council. The plant council can include these representatives as well as staff professionals, such as human resources, and the facility's senior management team. Like a division council, the mission of the plant council must be defined and boundaries established. The plant council must meet on a regular basis, with minutes published, and often with the assistance of a neutral facilitator.

THE MONDRAGON MODEL

The largest model for democratic decision making in a nongovernmental body is the Mondragon cooperatives in the Basque region of Spain. Mondragon has over 22,000 employee-owners. Mondragon includes a wide range of activities, including banking, farming, retail sales, machining, operation of a foundry, a university, and a construction company.

Each entity in the Mondragon model has a constitution that defines its mission and boundaries. The constitution establishes the governing council *(Junta Rectora)* that is elected by the member/workers in the organization. The managers who administer business activities report to the governing council, having a voice in council decisions, but no vote.

Managers conduct their own council for addressing day to day working issues. In addition to the governing council, a Mondragon organization will often have an audit committee (see Chapter 5) to keep an independent eye on how the organization conducts business.

Each business unit has its own governing council with its own elected representatives from its divisions and teams. Business units are banded together under a general assembly *(Asembla General)* for major groupings. All the members of each governing council belong to the general assembly.

THE MEANING OF CONSENSUS

Most people have two clear models of decision making that they have experienced, either an autocratic approach or a majority rules approach. In the autocratic model, the person with the formal decision-making authority makes the decision and tells people what to do. There are variations on this model, where the person with the authority asks for people's ideas or their questions, but the bottom line is still the same.

The majority rules model is seen in government, and is viewed positively by some and negatively by others. In this model, the majority has its way and the minority's interests may not be met at all.

Consensus decision making is a very different third path. In consensus decision making, participants do not vote on issues. Voting often creates winners and losers, and this will polarize a group. It becomes hard for a group to work together when some people feel that their interests are not being met.

Building consensus means entering into dialogue within the group until everyone in the group can have enough buy-in with the decision to go along with it. Achieving consensus does not mean that everyone in the group agrees with 100 percent of the groups decisions. What consensus means is that at any time, every member of the group is at least 70% comfortable with each decision the group has made.

Consensus is reached through discussion. In this discussion, it is very important that everyone understand the objectives that the group is attempting to meet by making a decision. The discussion needs to continue until everyone can at least give a 70 percent buy-in to the decision.

For consensus decision making to work, there must be some degree of cohesion within the group. This means that people want to be part of the group, and share in the purpose of the group. Each person must feel they have an equal voice in the decision-making process, and be willing to commit the time and energy to be in dialogue. Participants must start with a willingness to cooperate and a willingness to learn to make consensus-based decisions and to practice this skill.

There are common problems that organizations can encounter in building a consensus-based decision making process. First, outspoken individuals can dominate the group or organization. Individuals can choose to block an action by taking a strong opposing position to a proposal. This blocking is appropriate if the individual really has legitimate heartburn with a particular proposal, but blocking can become a tactic that causes the group to become dysfunctional over time. If members are too verbose, the process can become too time consuming and can cause participants to burn out.

TOOLS TO SUPPORT CONSENSUS DECISION MAKING

Consensus decision making can be expedited in any organization through the use of two decision-making tools. The first is a decision-making flow process called rational decision making and the second is a process known as nominal group technique.

Rational Decision Making

In rational decision making, a group must first define the objectives that it is seeking to achieve in making a decision. The objectives may be to meet a deadline, save money, speed up delivery, improve quality, or any of a host of possible outcomes. It is always best to discuss and achieve consensus regarding the objectives first. When objectives are discussed in a group setting, everyone understands what the other people in the group wish to achieve by making the decision. Developing a consensus about what is to be achieved makes it relatively easy to go on to developing a consensus about which choice best meets the group's objectives.

Objectives can be seen as those that must be achieved and those that it would be good to have. The objectives that are musts will have a high priority in deciding whether or not a particular choice should or should not be kept in the running. In some cases, it is useful to identify which of the "good to have" objectives is the most important of that type.

After the group has agreed on what it is trying to achieve and which objectives must be achieved and which would be "good to have," the group is ready to go on to identifying choices. It is important that everyone in the group have their voice in identifying alternatives. If someone has an idea and is not allowed to put it out for consideration, they will resist the overall process.

List the choices for all to see, then screen them through the objectives that must be achieved. If an alternative cannot meet one of these must objectives, then that alternative should be eliminated. Next, look at the choices that made it through this screening process. Ask, which of these best meets the remaining "like to have" criteria?

As a group, seek to agree on which alternative best meets the objectives, but before the group finalizes the decision, the question should be asked, what can go wrong with this? If the group finds no show stopper on this question, then they are ready to proceed with implementation.

Nominal Group Technique

Nominal group technique (NGT) offers a quick method for finding out where people stand on an issue without becoming involved in a whole lot of discussion. In NGT, ideas or choices are listed for the whole group to see and each person then ranks the choices, giving the highest rank to the choice they think is best.

For example, a group needs to choose methods to cut costs for the organization. They brainstorm a list of ideas. The group can take time to discuss and clarify the ideas, and even allow for some lobbying. Then, each person takes a piece of paper and places the numbers 5, 4, 3, 2, and 1 on their page. Working individually, each person evaluates the list and places what they consider to be the best idea next to the 5, the next best next to the 4, and so forth. Then, someone collects all the papers and tallies the ranking (number of votes) given to each idea. A score of 5 counts as 5 votes for an idea. A score of 4 counts as 4 votes for an idea.

What distinguishes NGT from majority rule is that every person gets an opportunity to identify several options they think are best. In most cases, at least some part of every person's opinion gets included in the short list of best options.

This process can be speeded up greatly if the group uses a system where each person has a voting pad that is tied to a computer that will tally the rankings immediately and display them on a computer screen that can be projected onto a screen.

THE LIFE CYCLE OF A GROUP

No group will last forever. Group members come and go and change in many ways over time. The challenges for a group can change greatly from the time that it is first formed until the time when it is disbanded.

Malcolm and Hulda Knowles developed a comprehensive introduction to group dynamics that summarized about a dozen studies of the life cycles of groups. Most of these studies recognize that a group changes over time.

In a first phase, groups work to define their mission and their boundaries, seeking to clarify what role each person is to play. The energy level may be high, if this is a new opportunity for the group members or if there is an urgent need that the group is being formed to address.

After the initial excitement of forming the group and defining roles and boundaries, the group will probably experience some internal conflict as the roles require clarification and as people get used to each other. Differences in personalities, communication styles, language, and values come to the surface and become irritants. Conflicts can be minor or serious. At this stage, a conflict resolution tool, such as the Thomas- Kilman instrument, or a personality type indicator such as the Myers- Briggs instrument can be of value to overcoming the tension.

Over time, the group will settle into some degree of cohesion as people learn what they can expect from one another. Trust develops based on cooperation. If this cohesion does not come about, the group will become dysfunctional and will cease to be an effective body. During this time of cohesion, the group may become highly productive, capable of a wide range of activities.

When the group members change, due to additions to the group or some group member having to end their membership in the group, then the group must go back to an earlier stage in which members readjust to the new members. It is important to help new members quickly accept the mission of the group, the boundaries, and the group's ways of doing business, or for the group to make modifications based on new members' needs.

CONSENSUS DECISION MAKING VERSUS GROUP THINK

Dr. Irving Janis has conducted research into what he has called the "group think" phenomenon. In "group think" individuals are concerned with holding on to their position or membership in a group to the extent that they consciously or unconsciously censor their opinions in order to maintain the cohesion of the group. In a "group think" situation, group members may have doubts about decisions that they decide not to express. Group members may decide that it is disloyal to the group to ask questions or express dissenting views.

Consensus decision making is not an effort to create group think. Participants in a consentaneous group (a group that is governed by consensus) give buy-in to a decision, but must be free to express when a possible action gives them serious concern.

The use of a rational decision-making process is one method to help avoid group think. The rational decision making process forces the group to address the question of what can go wrong? before finalizing a group decision.

The nominal group technique likewise helps combat "group think." In NGT, each participant expresses their ranking individually and no one knows who gave the choices which ranking. This encourages people to call it as they see it without concern that their view will be considered to be rocking the boat.

APPENDIX:
Opportunities for Praxis

1. Where does your organization stand in terms of organizing around teams, division councils, all-college councils, or along the Mondragon model? What would be the easiest next step for your organization to move in this direction?

2. Where does your organization already use consensus decision-making methods?

3. In rational decision making, why is it preferable to establish consensus around the objectives to be achieved before moving on to discussing the choices?

4. What do you think would be the greatest advantages of using nominal group technique with a council form of governance?

5. What would be signs that an organization is suffering from "group think"?

7

Empowerment and Planning

In an empowering organization, people in the workforce are engaged in both the strategic and tactical planning for the organization. Employees will be directly involved in the tactical planning for their specific part of the organization, and may be either directly involved in strategic planning, or involved through a representative process.

Seven Step Path to Empowerment
1. Create champions.
2. Involve people in planning the change.
3. Create team leaders.
4. Educate the workforce.
5. Change the support system.
6. Practice consensus decision making.
➤ *7. Involve people in strategic and tactical planning.*

Participative planning may initially sound cumbersome and awkward for an organization. Plans can be quickly developed by one or two people, but a participative process will require more time. What is well proven, however, by the Japanese approach to participative planning, is that the extra time spent in participative planning is greatly returned to the organization by the commitment given to the plan during implementation by the people who developed the plan. Those who create tend to support. Fast planning conducted by a select few usually results in a plan that falters in the implementation stage due to a lack of commitment by the many people who must take actions to bring the plan to fruition.

The initial concern about the time-consuming nature of participative planning is offset when an organization develops a clear and efficient process for planning. When an effective planning process exists, the organization has a planning pattern to follow that will speed up the participative planning activities.

This chapter will examine patterns for tactical and strategic planning that will enable a group to move efficiently, and also examines issues regarding the use of a facilitator in planning and who needs to be a part of a planning effort.

STRATEGIC PLANNING

Although some organizations drift without any particular strategic plan, most successful organizations use strategic planning as a fundamental tool for establishing the broad objectives that must be achieved for the organization to succeed in its mission.

In autocratic settings, strategic plans will be developed by a small select group that controls the organization. Democratic organizations can employ strategic planning, with a broader group of people involved.

Steps in Effective Strategic Planning
1. Establish a vision.
2. Identify gaps between the "as is" and the vision.
3. Scan for potential changes.
4. Establish strategic objectives.
5. Identify major enabling actions (tactics).

In its most basic form, the major steps for strategic planning are the same for autocratic or democratic settings. The planners must (1) look at what they think the future trends are in their business or field, (2) establish a vision for what their organization needs to become, (3) identify the gaps between the current status and the vision, (4) establish broad strategic objectives that will close the gaps and address issues found in the scanning process, and (5) identify enabling actions (tactics) that will accomplish the strategic objectives.

Think about the Future

To start the strategic planning process, a planning team needs to be organized that will begin by establishing what is known or believed to be true or probable about the future, as it relates to the specific organization. Demographic trends, consumer buying trends, expected technology, or any other information that will influence the organization's future needs to be identified. In addition, the team should consider what they believe their competitors will be doing to better position themselves in this possible future, and what their core client or customer base will want in this future. This process might take a bit of data gathering, and could possibly draw on the expertise of some futurist consultants.

When the information is amassed, the team needs to establish some time for this information to soak in. Each strategic planning team member should consider the impact of this information on the organization and begin to develop their own ideas as to how the organization needs to position itself for the future.

Establishing a Vision

In a democratic organization, it is essential for people to have a common shared vision about what the organization is seeking to become. This vision inspires, unites, and serves as a compass pointing to the "true north" for the organization when decisions need to be made.

The appropriate leadership team will need to set aside some time to dream new dreams and create the vision. Often, this is done by a simple exercise in which the leaders are able to describe how the organization will look in five, ten, or twenty-five years. Each person shares their ideas of what the organization would have accomplished in the ensuing years, how it has grown, what technology is used, how the people have prospered, and how the organization has changed. This basic exercise draws out visionary ideas and allows people to explore one another's thoughts about the future. From this exercise, the strategic planning team distills a vision for the organization.

Identify Gaps

With a vision established, the team next works to identify the gaps between where the organization currently is, and where the vision would place it in the future. Gaps may relate to the size of the organization, sales volume, market share, earnings, reputation, benefits, projects, or any other attributes.

The purpose of identifying gaps is not to throw cold water on the team after they have created a vision, but to quickly focus on the areas that are going to need the most work to turn the vision into reality. The team needs to develop a consensus of where the gaps are because the organization may need to refocus resources to close the gaps, and everyone will need to support this change, since it may not be easy. The identification of gaps can also be inspiring to people, since it raises the possibility of success, if key objectives can established that will effectively close the gaps that exist between the vision and the organization's "as is" condition.

Establishing Strategic Objectives

With the gaps established, the team needs to agree on strategic objectives that will enable the organization to close the gaps. Consensus on the strategic objectives is again vital to ensure commitment to reallocating resources and adhering to enabling actions (tactics). Without these strategic objectives, the organization will drift into the future without a clear path for achieving the vision, so the vision will most likely go unrealized.

The process for establishing the strategic objectives is often disarmingly simple. The team looks at a gap and says, what do we need to do about this? Then, based on their own knowledge and experience, they answer the question. In a few rare cases, the team may need to bring in someone with expert knowledge who can help answer the question as to what needs to be done.

Establishing what needs to be done is still only half of the task. The remaining issue is to establish what will be done. There may be several possible strategies for closing a gap. Which one will the group select? For example, the gap may deal with satisfying unhappy customers. There are multiple strategies for addressing this issue. Which one does the group want to use? This requires the team to consider it objectives, such as conserving finances, the time available, and the way that the decision might impact the organization. One option might be costly, but quick, with a major negative impact on the workforce. Another option might be slower, but less expensive, with little impact on the workforce. The best choice depends on the objectives that need to be met.

Establishing the strategic objectives does not mean planning how each objective will be implemented in detail. If the strategic planning team attempts to move into specific implementation, it has moved into the field of tactical planning, and is probably bumping into the boundaries of strategic planning. To cross this boundary may be moving into some group within the organization's boundaries, disempowering them.

TACTICAL PLANNING

Tactical plans are specific actions that the organization needs to take to support a strategic objective. Tactical plans are either derived from a strategic planning process, or are developed to handle day-to-day issues that arise in any organization.

An effective tactical planning process will work well at any of the organization levels modeled in Chapter 6, such as the team, in a council, or even at the large organization level, such as Mondragon.

The following list outlines the steps in effective tactical planning. When a group adheres to these steps and stays on task, the planning process can go very quickly.

Effective Tactical Planning
1. Understand the objective.
2. Develop an action plan.

3. Anticipate what might go wrong.
4. Plan how to head off possible problems.
5. Anticipate recovery steps.
6. Implement the plan and the recovery steps (as needed).

When a team meets together to develop a plan, there must be a consensus as to what the plan is to accomplish (step #1). The objective that the plan is to achieve should be clearly stated. If a team does not share a common view of what the plan is to accomplish, then the planning process will break down.

With the objective clear in everyone's minds, an action plan (step #2) must be established. The team should start by defining everything that needs to be done to accomplish the objective, and arranging these actions in the right sequence. If it is a complicated plan, then a critical path that outlines the most important steps should also be generated.

When the team has agreed on what the right steps in the plan should be and have arranged them in the right sequence, the next step is to determine who should be responsible for accomplishing each action item. Here is where participative planning proves its superiority to autocratic planning. The individuals or groups that must commit to the plan are present or represented and can make a commitment to own the action items.

Once ownership of each action item is established, then the group needs to agree on the deadlines for each step. It may be helpful to start by establishing the final deadline for implementation, and work from the end point back through each step in the plan to the beginning to establish time deadlines. This method allows you to see where there may be problems and where it may be necessary to work concurrently on various steps.

With agreement on what is to be done, who is to do it, and the deadlines for completion established, the group can move on to step 3, anticipating what might go wrong with the plan. Plans often fail because the planners assume that nothing will go wrong with their plan. If a team avoids asking this difficult question, then potential flaws in the plan will remain unmentioned and/or undetected that will cause problems in the implementation phase. Asking what can go wrong with a plan is another method to help ensure that the team is not slipping into group think (see Chapter 6).

The team needs to look at the plan and simply ask, what could go wrong? and make a list of what answers come from that question. Then, the group can quickly dismiss those possible problems that are of low probability of occurrence, or that have no real consequence even if they do occur. Hopefully, a group will not even spend time identifying these minutiae and will instead be disciplined to only look for the "show stoppers."

Once the team has honed down the things that can possibly go wrong to just the serious "show stoppers," the team moves on to step 4, planning how to head off these potential problems. The team needs to ask, what action can we take, or what barrier can we construct that will keep this problem from happening? An ounce of prevention is always worth a pound of cure, so it makes sense to figure out how to head off the problems at the pass before they can impact your plan or mix your metaphors.

Sometimes the team will find that there simply are not enough adequate actions that can be taken to ensure that a possible problem can be avoided. In this case, the team must move on to step 5 and have a recovery plan in place if the problem does occur. For example, in planning to ship a product in a truck, a team may plan how to avoid breakdowns and delays. But if a breakdown were to occur, the team should already know how that problem will be corrected. For serious problems that have a significant likelihood of happening, the team should know ahead of time how it will deal with the issue. This way, the team has covered all the bases and will be adequately prepared to recover from problems.

Finally, in step 6, the team needs to implement the tactical plan and track its progress. If possible problems do begin to occur, the team should be ready to implement a recovery plan. The team should review the progress of the plan and should recognize ahead of time if a deadline will not be met to have adequate time for the recovery actions.

A succinct, repeatable planning process that everyone on the team knows and uses will greatly speed up the team's tactical planning process. The ability to quickly develop workable plans is important in most organizational settings, so the need for rapid and reliable tactical planning is a serious issue. Effective tactical planning provides the organization with a nimble ability to respond to changes and a reliable method to achieve strategic objectives.

USING A FACILITATOR

In many planning settings, it is useful to the planners to bring in a neutral facilitator to lead the planning process, whether the planning is strategic or tactical. Using a facilitator allows everyone on the team to have the opportunity to participate equally. No team member has to be playing the scribe or trying to lead the process when each needs to be contributing the the content. Likewise, a facilitator can help ensure that no one person is overly dominant in the discussion. A facilitator will ensure that every person has the opportunity to speak on each issue and be open in committing to action steps.

In strategic planning, the facilitator will help the group identify the vision, and in clarifying the gaps between the vision and the current situations. From this process, the facilitator can involve the team members in developing crisp objectives that need to be accomplished and can prepare the team to create tactical plans that will achieve the strategic objectives.

For tactical planning, the facilitator can provide the mechanism for making sure that the important questions about what can go wrong are asked and answered by the team. No team member is diverted from thinking about what steps should be taken due to having to both lead the process and offer content information. The facilitator can also ensure that the planning information is captured on an easel to make it easy for all the team members to have a common understanding of what information is going into the plan.

For both strategic and tactical planning, the use of a neutral facilitator provides another important barrier to group think. The facilitator can make sure that the group does not practice self-censorship and can help ensure that dissenting opinions are voiced.

WHO SHOULD PLAN?

To be true to a participative system, careful consideration must be given to who needs to be involved in strategic and tactical planning. At the individual team level, it is usually preferable to involve the entire team in both types of planning activities, but at larger organizational levels there are several issues to consider.

Where a council form of governance exists, it is often best to involve only the council members in the strategic planning. This certainly becomes true as each member is representing a larger and larger part of the organization. However, Marvin Weisbord has conducted some excellent work in large-group strategic planning in a format that he calls a future search conference, that he outlines in his book, *Discovering Common Ground*. Weisbord's future search method allows a large group of people to work together in a visioning process that results in a strong common agreement as to the direction that an organization should pursue.

APPENDIX:
Opportunities for Praxis

1. How do the steps for strategic planning and tactical planning in this chapter match the current practices in your organization?

2. What changes will your organization need to make to practice an empowering approach to planning?

8

Perspectives on Democracy in the Workplace

Company cultures have been compromise by abuses of technology, bureaucracy, and authority. Democratic values came on sailing ships a long time before. We conserve our culture when we seek to extend these values in the workplace, to keep open a creative dialogue between individualism and the common good.

—Marvin Weisbord, *Productive Workplaces*

Organizational development and quality improvement efforts run into difficulties when the people implementing various changes really have very little vision about what they are trying to achieve. As the Roman philosopher Seneca noted, without a port to which to sail, any wind is the right one.

Too many change agents grasp some form of change that they have heard about and seek to implement it within their organization without really having a vision of what their organization needs to become. Many end up creating false empowerment of people by raising the expectation that the employees are really going to be involved in decision making. Involving employees only to improve quality or reduce costs soon leads to disenchantment among the workers.

To help change agents choose a path that will render the greatest benefit for the organization, it will be useful to take some time to tell the story of democracy and how this form of governance can function effectively in a competitive world market.

DEMOS + KRATIA

The fact that democracy originated in theory and in practice in ancient Greece is well known. What most people do not know is how it evolved among the Greeks and then seemed to appear out of nowhere in the minds of the American "Founding Fathers."

The important point about Greek democracy is that it evolved slowly over many decades. Democracy comes to us as a combination of two words, *demos*, meaning the people, and *kratia*, from *kratos*, meaning strength or power. Democracy means the strength is vested in the people, as opposed to other forms of government that the Greeks also utilized, such as autocracy, meaning strength in the one.

We associate democracy with the city-state of Athens, because it was in Athens that Kleisthenes introduced a series of reforms that reorganized the people into tribes that would have a vote on issues. Kleisthenes' reforms created a council, which served as an executive, and an assembly, which served as a legislative body.

The concept of balancing power between the executive and legislative bodies took a long time to develop, but it paid off for Athens during the series of wars she fought with Sparta. Additional reforms were introduced by Ephialtes and Pericles (around 460 B.C.) which expanded the role of the juries and courts, creating what was in essence a government that balanced power between an executive, a legislature, and the courts.

However, Athenian democracy was a democracy of the wealthy and the elite. Only men of Athens were allowed a vote, and the whole economic system was based on slave labor. Democracy in Athens was a series of struggles to maintain the balance of power created by democracy, which was often threatened by individuals or the mob.

Aristotle was raised in Greek society and was a critic of many forms of government. Above all, Aristotle warned against allowing the tyranny of the mob to become a city's form of governance. Aristotle favored the rule of a few well-educated people above other options. As experts such as John Dewey have noted, much of the American educational system has been built on Aristotle's views regarding separating the elite leadership from the common people.

The basic issue for democracy in ancient times was the struggle between participation and efficiency. Ancient democracies took days and days to reach a decision. Decisions that were reached one day might be overturned a few days later when the people attending the meeting might change. The autocracy, on the other hand, was very efficient. Decisions could be made quickly and with a clear purpose in mind.

Democratic forms of governance were not exclusive to Athens. Similar processes are believed to have existed in other city-states, such as Rhodes, but these have not received the attention of Athens because Athens produced great historians who documented her events.

The elements of democratic theory were an essential ingredient in Republican Rome. Rome had a Senate, which served as the legislative branch, and each year elected a pair of leaders who served as the executive branch. Courts were created from the Senate, and at times from other groups. Although the Roman republic did not create the same balance of power as had Athens, the concept was maintained. Even during the centuries of the emperors, the institutional trappings of a balance of power were important.

CITY-STATES

Democracy did not fare very well under the Roman Empire and did poorly during the Middle Ages. However, the idea began to come back to life in the eleventh century when Italian city-states, such as Pisa, Milan, Genoa, Arezzo, Bologna, Padua, and Siena, formed constitutions that provided for elections of councils to govern the cities.

Democracy began to make inroads in England in the 1640s in the time between the defeat of the Royalists and the rise of Cromwell's faction. The so-called "levelling movement" of this era sought to introduce the concept of political equality, advocating popular representative government.

IN AMERICA

In the decades prior to the American Revolution the concept of democracy in the form of a republic administered by the people was a popular concept in the American colonies as well as in England and on the Continent. It is difficult for most contemporary people to understand the intellectual soup of the eighteenth century. The educated elite of that era had a wide knowledge of classical literature and were well versed in the writings of the Middle Ages and the Enlightenment. Most of today's educated population is unaware of what the eighteenth century's educated people knew, having invested instead in learning the knowledge of the nineteenth and twentieth centuries.

The "Founding Fathers" of the American republic were well versed in the political theory of Greece and Rome. They knew about the successful use of democracy in the Italian city-states. The idea of governing a society by creating a balance of power was well known, since Britain was considered to be a balance between the crown, the House of Lords, and the courts. The American Constitution, which was eventually adopted built on the ancient Greek and the British model with a four-way balance of power between an executive branch (elected instead of enthroned), a Senate, a House, and a judicial branch.

In addition to their classical knowledge, the founders were very aware of the various democratic confederations that existed among the Native

American tribes that bordered the English colonies. Most of the tribes practiced participatory democracy in which anyone could speak in counsel and decisions were made in consensus. The new democratic system of the United States was a synthesis of Old World knowledge with new world experiences, as illustrated in Figure 8.1.

The Native American tribes along the western boundaries of the colonies had established a very sophisticated system of participatory democracy. At the village level, councils were held in which all could speak. At the tribal level, villages were represented by designated spokesmen. Elaborate confederacies were formed that linked multiple tribes into unions. These confederacies conducted formal meetings in which broad policies were established through consensus decision making. Founding Fathers, such as Benjamin Franklin, had extensive contact with the Native American confederacies. In fact, the confederacies often advised the colonials to form their own union.

The Albany Plan of Union, drafted by Benjamin Franklin, was a close copy of the Iroquois Confederacy. The Articles of Confederation built on the Albany Plan of Union, as the Constitution of the United States built on the Articles of Confederation. There is a clear flow from the Iroquois Nation's Confederacy to the American Constitution in philosophy of self-government and participatory democracy. However, the Founding Fathers were less democratic than the Native Americans, allowing only men to participate in the democractic process while also continuing the savage practice of slavery.

Figure 8.1
Creating the new democratic system.

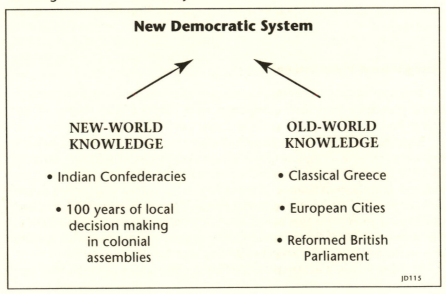

New Democratic System

NEW-WORLD KNOWLEDGE

- Indian Confederacies
- 100 years of local decision making in colonial assemblies

OLD-WORLD KNOWLEDGE

- Classical Greece
- European Cities
- Reformed British Parliament

JD115

Establishing and maintaining a balance of power was the key to creating democracy in the new nation, just as balancing power will be seen to be the key to creating democracy in the workplace.

The issue of democracy in the workplace began in the late 1800s and had grown into a movement for "industrial democracy" by the early 1900s. Many of the well-known contributors to business management theory were supporters of the industrial democracy movement, including people such as Henry Gantt and Mary Parker Follett. However, when modern business educators discuss business theory, they rarely acknowledge the extensive industrial democracy movement, for some strange reason.

In general, business theorists will suggest that democracy cannot work in industry because people will not vote themselves to take risks or to eliminate inefficient practices. This is a reasonable criticism. However, there are some notable examples that refute this belief and that bear investigating as models for democracy in the workplace.

MODELS FOR DEMOCRACY IN THE WORKPLACE

There are at least five different models for implementing democracy in the workplace. Each has different historical perspectives and strengths and weaknesses. The first model consists of situations where enlightened senior management attempts to introduce democratic elements into the workplace. The second model comes from situations where people start and expand an organization based on democratic principles. The third model occurs when employees buy an existing business. A fourth model comes about as a result of a redesign of a workplace, using the methods of the Tavistock Institute. The fifth model might be called "low-intensity democracy," where democratic practices are slowly introduced into an autocratic setting.

"Enlightened Management"

Two outstanding examples of managers who sought to introduce democratic principles into their companies were Henry Nunn, owner of the Nunn-Bush shoe company, and the Canadian businessman, H. B. Wilson.

Beginning in 1915, Nunn launched what he called "the struggle to build democracy in this company" by involving craftsmen in decision making. In 1919 the company welcomed an intramural union that provided the workers with elected leaders to represent them on the company's board of directors. In partnership with the union, the company created a share-production plan for wages based on a 36 percent return of total sales to the workers, instead of the piece rate or hourly wage. The union leaders also participated in the process of setting management's salaries.

In Nunn's view, management and labor must respect one another and recognize their mutual interdependence for the good of the whole. Labor works *with* management, not *for* management, according to Nunn, and both labor and management are paid by the customer who buys the product. "Democracy in industrial relations involves keeping workers advised of all actions at the top level and giving them a voice and a vote in decisions made," in Nunn's words.

In 1935, during the depths of the Great Depression, Nunn and his union officials adopted the share-production plan and a method for providing the employees (who were called associates back then) with weekly pay checks. While management hires new employees, the union must also accept them into membership after a thirty-day trial period. If the union does not accept the person, then he cannot stay with the company. In addition to the belief in a "cooperative partnership," Nunn also placed a high priority on providing job security. As workers obtained seniority they became part of a no-lay-off core of associates, which was also extended to handicapped people of lower seniority.

All these actions made sound business sense, according to Nunn. He pointed out how the workers are in the best position to save money for the company and how a cooperative climate creates continuity. In the forty-eight years of his leadership, Nunn-Bush had no strikes or arbitrations in their factory of 1100 workers.

Writing in 1961, Nunn explained to other managers how he and his union leaders and managers created their participative environment over a thirty-year period. He compared his profit-sharing approach to the Scanlon plan (introduced in 1945), and also critiques other participative programs, such as those at Proctor and Gamble and at Hormel, but faulted them for failing to relinquish their "traditional prerogative of arbitrary power."

Henry Nunn stands almost alone as a capitalist who introduced industrial democracy in the Woodrow Wilson era, shepherded it through the Great Depression, and brought the concept into the postwar era. His trailblazing efforts were matched in Canada by H. B. Wilson.

Wilson challenged the need for continuing to have a division between the managers and the managed, advocating worker representation on boards and participation in the local work areas. Although there would still be a role for unions, Wilson hoped that participation and representation would end the adversarial relationship between management and unions.

One compelling reason for supporting industrial democracy, according to Wilson, is efficiency. A hierarchical structure devotes much of its energy to controlling people, but a participative system, based on respect for human dignity, focuses organizational resources on doing the work. However, industrial democracy is not just about increasing productivity; in Wilson's view, "it is a way of living and developing during the work day."

Wilson cautioned against programs that provide for "token participation to manipulate employees into thinking they are part of the team" while actually retaining an autocratic structure. "Contemporary autocratic management attempts to manipulate employees toward controlled innovation. Industrial democracy opens up the possibility for innovation to all employees and creates a free environment which encourages innovative thought."

Examining the traditional managerial role, Wilson observed that groups can set goals democratically and avoid the time wasted in constant reorganization of the company, which occupies much of management's time. Management's emphasis on organization only creates walls to cooperation, which must be broken down, according to Wilson. A democratic system can provide good control, in Wilson's view, and many technical issues, such as coordination of work flow, can be handled by technical experts who are not bosses. Furthermore, when it comes to introducing new technology, Wilson argued that worker input to technological changes helps avoid the errors often made by managers. In short, there is little that managers do that cannot be done and done better by the workers, according to Wilson.

Greenfield Democracy

Business managers speak of new start-up plants as greenfield sites, for obvious reasons. In the same manner, there are models of greenfield democracy where employees start up their own businesses and build some form of democracy into their governance process.

The most outstanding example of the greenfield democracy model is the Mondragon organization in the Basque region of Spain. Mondragon was formed by a group of local people who needed to create jobs for their community. The guiding figure for this group has been a Catholic Priest, Don Jose Maria Arizmendiarrieta, who first set up a League for Education and Culture in 1948 in the Mondragon community. Building from the people in this educational movement, collectively owned businesses were created.

William F. Whyte and Kathleen Whyte conducted field research at Mondragon in the 1980s. They reported that the complex had developed many factories, one of the largest banking systems in Spain, a research and development wing, an agricultural section, and an extensive system to support these programs. Approximately 19,000 people are currently active in the Mondragon cooperative.

Mondragon practices a combination of representative democracy, town meetings, and participative activities. Managers of the cooperatives are approved by the workers. Each co-op has a general assembly for review of business and mini counsels to facilitate internal communications. Major changes in organization are subject to a total vote by all the co-op members.

Frank Adams and Gary Hansen have written extensively on the steps for starting a greenfield democratic workplace. Adams and Hansen have provided a comparison of commercial characteristics of industry under capitalism, socialism, and workers' cooperation as part of their explanation of the fundamentals of workplace democracy. They have examined the important characteristics of membership in worker-owned and controlled enterprises, such as volunteerism, proportionality of pay, participation in decision making, and awareness of what ownership means.

The Employees Buy the Company

Employees banding together to buy their company continues to be an option for moving toward democracy in the workplace. In addition to the well known employee purchases of companies, such as United Airlines and AVIS car rental, there are many companies in which employees own major shares of stock and have increased their influence.

A quick list of companies where employees hold at least a fourth of the stock includes Morgan Stanley, Stone & Webster, Oregon Steel Mills, Grumman, Rockwell International, Century Telephone, Herman Miller, Kroger, McDonnell Douglas, and Proctor & Gamble.

However, employee ownership does not necessarily equate with employee democracy. In many cases the employees own large portions of the organization's stocks but are willing to be managed along the traditional autocratic paradigm.

As the number of employee purchased companies expands, the opportunity for introducing democracy will likewise grow. When Polaroid Corp. established an Employee Stock Option Plan that gave 19 percent of the company to employees, a position was created on the Board of Directors for a middle manager to represent employee interests. China Books & Publishing became employee owned in 1991. The employees will elect the board of directors and vote on the company's budget and on policy matters.

It is probable that the expansion of employee buyouts of companies will result in more democratic systems of governance based on a balance of power scheme, where hired management shares power with employee councils.

Redesign Efforts

Another path towards democracy has resulted from the sociotechnical systems redesign process developed at the Tavistock Institute in Great Britain. Much of Tavistock's work grew out of writings of Eric Trist regarding autonomous work groups in British coal mines. The Tavistock coal mining studies were conducted from 1954 to 1958, using a process to analyze the technical work being performed and the human relations issues related to performing the work. To best match people's needs with the technology for mining, Trist and his design team, along with management and union leaders, agree to form "self-regulating primary work groups" that oversaw their own production work. They found that this system enabled the supervisors to focus their attention in other areas.

P. G. Hurst complied a technical follow-up on Trist's work, providing details regarding research methods and findings. Hurst observed the operational conditions under which the Tavistock group found that autonomous teams can develop and thrive. First, the work task itself must be an independent whole. Second, the work needs to be performed within an identifiable physical boundary, which provides territory the group can "own." Another important point is that control of the work must be linked to measurable performance indicators.

Marvin Weisbord has been a successful advocate of the work redesign process in the United States. Weisbord has written an excellent text on leading the redesign process and is producing a videotape series that illustrates the high level of participation that occurs in a redesigned work culture.

However, a high level of participation in day-to-day decision making among autonomous work groups does not in and of itself constitute democracy in the workplace. The success of the work groups in self-determination needs to be elevated to higher levels of decision making within the organization. On the other hand, the success of the redesign efforts should by no means be dismissed as insignificant. It may well turn out that these redesign efforts are an essential step along the road toward building democratic workplaces.

"Low-Intensity" Democracy

The term *"low-intensity" democracy* has been recently introduced by political scientists to describe the introduction of democracy into autocratic nations. The trappings of democracy, such as elections, begin to appear, but the underlying problems of a strong willed military or a powerful ruling family may still continue to exist.

Low-intensity democracy may be another important step that countries need to take to evolve into a fully democratic balance of power. Indeed, it could be argued that England had to work through many decades of low-intensity democracy before the current system of parliamentary democracy evolved.

Many workplaces have experimented and continue to experiment with low-intensity democracy. The most notable example in the past was the creation of "Whitley Councils" in England and America during the First World War. These councils permitted employees to elect representatives and to have greater input into the decision-making process. These councils largely died out following the war, but made vital contributions to the war effort.

There are two contemporary efforts toward low-intensity democracy in the workplace today. One involves the increase in joint union and management cooperative efforts and the other involves the reintroduction of elected councils into work groups that are not unionized.

By and large, American unions will support the introduction of a joint union and management effort to improve quality and lower costs if the system recognizes the legitimate right of the union to exist and to represent the employee's interests. When management is willing to create a balance of power, sharing decision making with the elected representatives of the employees' union, then the interests of the union have been met.

Most workplaces, however, do not have unions. It is against the labor laws for companies to set up councils and appoint employees to represent their peer's point of view. However, it is legal for organizations to give their people freedom to form caucus groups and to elect people to represent the employee's interests without going to the length of formally establishing a union.

The low-intensity democracy alternative is a model for introducing democracy into strongly entrenched autocratic systems. Development of successful democracy may take several decades.

KEYS TO SUCCESS

The key to success in the creation of democracy in the workplace is for all stakeholders to have representation in the governance of the organization. Democracy is a state of governance that organizations can evolve into or it can be designed in from the start. In either case, there must be a dynamic tension between some form of executive and council functions.

In a schools system, democracy means involving the students, teachers, administrators, parents, and local officials in making decisions. In a business, the stakeholders must include the investors, management, and workers. In a social agency, the stake holders include the funding agency, the management, the social workers, and the clients.

Max Elden has provided astute criticism of the organizational development field that tends to support any form of greater involvement for workers, but that may not be designed to move the organization toward a more democratic form of governance. Greater involvement for the purpose of enriching the investors while excluding the people who perform the day-to-day work from real participation will bear little fruit in the long run. The whole quality circle movement in America withered primarily for this reason.

The success of the movement toward democratization depends first and foremost on the vision of those who are creating and tending the garden.

If the gardener's vision is limited to the introduction of team efforts that lack any connection with a movement toward democracy, then the results will be weak. When the gardener has a vision, the key elements of democratization can be phased in over time, or planted in a short amount of time.

The rest of this book will focus on steps and methods to introduce democratic practices into existing organizations, in a manner that coincides with the low-intensity democracy model. Many of the methods recommended for this approach can also be implemented in organizations that are employee-owned, green-field democracies, or redesigned structures as enhancements to the existing democratic practices.

APPENDIX:
Opportunities for Praxis

1. What are examples in your organization where balances of power exist?

2. What is your management's opinion of cooperation and involvement of employees in decision making?

3. Which of these various approaches to democratizing the workplace would work best in your organization?

9

Adult Education
and Workplace Democracy

> Dominating, autocratic control is the technique of ignorance
> and inability to lead in industry and business—and disastrous
> in the end. Just as democracy is a more civilized method of
> leadership in government, so it is, equally, with other groups.
> —Leland Bradford and Ronald Lippitt,
> *Building A Democratic Work Group*

The inter-relationship between education and democracy in society and in the workplace has been a core issue for adult educators ever since adult education emerged as a distinct field of study. From the earliest pioneers, through the rapid growth in the 1930s and 1940s and into the present day, many adult educators maintain a primary or partial interest in how education grows and reinforces democratic practices in the workplace, in local government, and on the national level.

Concern about industrial autocracy was being expressed among educators in the early years of the twentieth century, and American educators had already split into two camps prior to the start of the First World War.

One camp was headed by the primary creators of vocational training in the United States, David Sneden and Charles Prosser, who based their views about industrial education on a model in Imperial Germany in which separate vocational schools provided specific training for factory workers. Beginning in junior high school, students were "differentiated" into separate programs based on their "probable destines." As Sneden said, "Having once conceived of the citizen as we should like to have him, we can work back to find the numberless specific forms of training by which we can produce this type." Vocational education would produce people immediately ready to work in factories, which was beneficial to both the students and the industrialists.

In the other camp were educators who believed that workers should be educated to change the system of autocratic control. Among these were John Dewey, Ida Tarbell, and George Herbert Mead, who were all active in the National Vocational Guidance Association, which split form Charles Prosser's National Society for the Promotion of Industrial Education in 1913 over these issues.

Foremost among the advocates for democracy in education and industry was John Dewey, who summarized his thoughts on this subject in his 1916 publication, *Democracy and Education*. Dewy suggested that our current paradigm for education is based on the belief of Aristotle in a hierarchical society. Liberal education was perceived by Aristotle to be reserved for the male power elite, while slaves, and craftsmen, and women received training in specific tasks. This training provided economically valuable skills but no development in planning, organizing, and decision making, which are needed for self-government.

If the United States continued along the path of Sneden and Prosser, Dewey foresaw a divided society in which workers would have no involvement or responsibility for their work. This "would give to the masses a narrow technical trade education for specialized callings, carried on under the control of others." Regarding the situation in industry, Dewey observed that "in the economic region, control remains external and autocratic. Hence the split between inner mental action and outer physical action of which the traditional distinction between the liberal and the utilitarian is the reflex. An education which should unify the disposition of the members of society would do much to unify society itself."

Dewey proposed a melding of technical and liberal education to give workers the means to participate, "to become masters of their industrial fate." Furthermore, Dewey saw a need to provide a broader knowledge base to workers so that they could learn new skills when old ones became obsolete. However, Dewey saw a major obstacle to his goal in the presence of an autocracy in the country that had "a conscious object to prevent the development of freedom and responsibility" among the laboring classes.

THE 1920S

In the 1920s, the field of adult education in the United States began to develop a clear identity with professionals who saw their work as a profession with definable boundaries. One of the major issues for adult education in the 1920s was the issue of forming and sustaining democratic behaviors in the wide public arena and in the workplace.

Speaking at the dedication of the Milwaukee Extension Building for adult education for the University of Wisconsin in 1929, Glenn Frank stated, "This adult education building is located on one of the hottest firing lines of democracy. A valid democracy is impossible without a vital education." Frank's message was considered important enough within the adult education community to be included in the first issue of *The Journal of Adult Education*. Frank considered adult education to be central to the reform of the American educational system, and he believed that this reform would be "fundamental to the increase, the enrichment, and the moral unification of American democracy."

Marker Parker Follett was a major contributor to adult education and the issue of workplace democracy in the 1920s. Follett was active in vocational education and business education in America and Great Britain. In a 1927 paper entitled "The Psychology of Consent and Participation," Follett contended that democracy means far more than mere representation and consent to actions, but must include the active participation of the people in thinking and in cofunctioning. Citing several industrial examples of participative democracy, Follett observed that participation can be obtained in three ways: "by an organization which provides for it, by a daily management which recognizes and acts on the principle of participation, and by a method of settling differences, or a method of dealing with the diverse contributions of men very different in temperament, training, and attainments."

Individual and group needs must be joined, Follett suggested, to have effective participation. Individuals must have a "consciousness of unity" where they feel responsibility to themselves and to the group. This can then lead unions to join with management to solve industrial problems, in Follett's view.

THE 1930S

The Great Depression, which overshadowed the entire decade of the 1930s, dealt a crushing blow to industries, labor, and industrial democracy alike. In an era of failing business and brutal labor and management disputes, much ground was lost in creating democracy in the American workplace. Clearly it was the field of adult education that sustained a continued focus on developing industrial democracy and adult educators who were the champions of democracy during this decade of depression and developing fascism.

When Americans looked to Europe, they saw little to confirm the movement toward democracy. While British efforts to democratize the workplace fell to the same economic plague, the Germans and the Italians began to pull themselves out of the economic nightmare through autocratic governments and autocratic industry.

The challenge to democracy from fascism was a primary force in expanding the adult education movement as seen in the contributions of three adult educators from this era, Dorothy Hewitt, Moses Coady, and Eduard

Lindeman.

It was in this context of failed democracies in Europe and growing despotism in Germany, Italy, and Spain that Dorothy Hewitt wrote her 1937 guidebook for adult education, *Adult Education: A Dynamic for Democracy*. Confronted with a growing profascist movement in America, Hewitt cites "the imperative need for revitalizing of the spirit of democracy" to "resolve the age-old paradox of the individual in society in terms of freedom for the individual in the midst of restraint conducive to the common welfare of all."

The answer to the need for revitalizing democracy would be found in adult education, according to Hewitt. As a nation, "collectively tired from the long and unsuccessful battle" with the Great Depression, Hewitt observed that the forces of democracy were at low ebb. "To strengthen and invigorate the dynamic for democracy" must become a key role of education.

One of the places where adult learning could provide support for democracy, Hewitt believed, was in the workplace where individual responsibility must be increased. Hewitt hoped that "autocracy in business and industry, through the domination of small controlling groups" would be "replaced by more cooperative procedures with a lessening of the tension between employees and employers."

Another proponent of adult education and industrial democracy in the 1930s was Moses Coady, a Jesuit priest and professor at Xavier University in Nova Scotia. Coady began working with miners in the 1920s to establish study clubs as "an effort to educate the people by assisting them to become masters of their own economic destiny."

Coady's educational movement for economic self-determination expanded in 1929 to involve Xavier University in "education of the fishermen; giving them a voice in formulating the policies relating to their industry; initiating them in a program of consumers' and producers' cooperation."

Adult education was viewed by Coady as the key to democracy and to economic self-determination, as he expressed in his 1939 book, *Masters of Their Own Destiny*. Adult education should focus first on economic learning toward the creation of labor-owned cooperatives. "It is good pedagogy from several viewpoints, to begin with the economic phase," Coady argued. "A man learns best when his interests are keenest and his needs determine his interest."

As an example of the educational movement, Coady cited a group of fishermen involved in an adult education program who built their own lobster factory cooperative in 1923 that showed a $10,000 surplus in 1935. Coady believed that through the adult educational process, people are given the perception and tools they need to control their own economic circumstances. He noted, "as the economic power and control of the people increase, they can create for themselves instruments that will permit them to voice their own case and cause. Thus will they be enabled to play a more effective part in building the new democratic society."

Eduard Lindeman, known by his contemporaries as "The Democratic Man," also expressed concerns regarding democracy in the workplace. In 1929 Lindeman suggested that companies that had been involved in participative management processes could be used as models for dealing with broader social issues.

Stephen Brookfield organized many of Lindeman's journal publications into a single volume in 1987. In a 1935 article on "Re-Affirming the Democratic Process," Lindeman identified industrial democracy as a critical focal point for creating democracy in society. "Any person who presumes to talk of democracy, and talks about saving our liberties while at the same time attempting to defeat every move toward economic democracy, is either a very naive person or a hypocrite," Lindeman observed. In a 1938 article on "Group Work and Democracy," Lindeman lamented the lack of scientific methods for creating "further democratization of our economic system."

In addition to these three major leaders in adult education, other adult educators were also engaged in sustaining democracy during the depression. Everett Martin and Charles Mann both published articles in *The Journal of Adult Education* concerning the role of adult education in developing and maintaining democratic processes.

THE 1940S

As America entered the Second World War, there was a great willingness among labor and management leaders to cooperate together to achieve major breakthroughs in factory productivity. Chapter 10 will provide details on this era of union and management cooperation.

The war years also introduced a new era in which Eduard Lindeman's concern about the lack of scientific methods for furthering workplace democracy would begin to be addressed. By the end of the war, four researchers published significant studies that dealt with creating participative workplace. Elton Mayo, at Harvard University, focused on a review of the Hawthorne experiments; Kurt Lewin offered his theory of organization leadership styles; and Leland Bradford and Ronald Lippitt shared their observations about how to develop democratic work groups.

In 1945, Elton Mayo published his review of several studies, including the Hawthorne experiments in a work called *The Social Problems of an Industrial Civilization*. In this work, Mayo advocated democracy in the workplace that would provide "logical and purposive control from above, spontaneous and cooperative control from below."

Mayo began this work by reviewing social theories and observations by the French social philosophers, Frederic LePlay and Emile Durkheim, which focus on the group behavior of people. Employing the facts of group behavior from observations in controlled settings and from social theory, Mayo rejected social and economic theory that is based on individuals acting purely in their own interests. A primary thesis in Mayo's work was that the misguided belief in individuals acting in their own interests (such as in the works of David Ricardo and Thomas Hobbes) falsely justifies the "need for a Leviathan, a powerful State, which by the exercise of unique authority shall impose order on the rabble."

Referring to the Hawthorne experiments test room, Mayo reminds his reader that the six workers became a team, and the productivity continued to improve despite the experimental conditions because the participants "were happy in the knowledge that they were working without coercion from above or limitation from below." Based on his research findings, Mayo emphasized his belief that one of the major concerns for managers "must be that of organizing teamwork, that is to say, developing and sustaining cooperation."

In 1945, Kurt Lewin, a German social scientist who had immigrated to America, published his theory of organization leadership styles in an article called "The Practicality of Democracy." Based on studies in education, public service, and manufacturing, Lewin proposed that leaders would assume one of three styles: autocratic, laissez-faire, or democratic.

Both autocracy and democracy require leadership, according to Lewin, whereas laissez-faire is an absence of leadership. Autocracy and democracy stress discipline and group performance. Democracy and laissez-faire are similar in the freedom they give to group members to act on their own motivation. However, Lewin stressed, the three styles are not a linear continuum, meaning that democracy does not fall between autocracy and laissez-faire management.

Lewin offered data from manufacturing studies to show that participative decision making would increase production. He also pointed out that controlled experiments indicated that little improvement would be achieved in performance if workers were only allowed to discuss issues and not allowed to make decisions. Lewin noted that relaxing pressure in the workplace only means shifting to a "softer form of autocracy, or perhaps to laissez-faire management, but not to democracy."

According to Lewin, democratic methods are superior when management needs to bring about change. "Group decisions provide a background of motivation, where the individual is ready to co-operate as a member of the group, more or less independent of his personal inclinations."

Leland Bradford and Ronald Lippitt also published their observations about democratic and autocratic management in their 1945 work, "Building A Democratic Work Group" published in *Personnel* magazine. Bradford and Lippitt found that "supervisors who can develop democratic work teams

by encouraging their employees to participate in supervision have few production and morale problems. In the autocratic work atmosphere, on the
other hand, production suffers because the employees' basic needs for
'belongingness' is blocked." While noting that almost everyone in America
favors democracy, the commitment to the principle seems to evaporate
when discussing the workplace. "This tragically curious contrast of beliefs
symbolizes the confusions, inabilities, and lack of knowledge which prevent most supervisors from developing efficient work groups. Dominating,
autocratic control is the technique of ignorance and inability to lead in
industry and business—and disastrous in the end. Just as democracy is a
more civilized method of leadership in government, so it is, equally, with
other groups."

Among the professional adult educators, the war years offered a great
deal of opportunity to reflect on the relationship between democracy and
adult education. "Democracy In Crisis," a panel discussion published in
June of 1941, involved nine adult education leaders including Lyman
Bryson from Columbia University, Eleanoir Coit from the American Labor
Education Service, J.E. Sproul of the National YMCA, and Author Bestor,
President of the Chautauqua Institute. The panel discussion showed how
adult educators considered democracy to be a primary area of emphasis
in their field. Sproul noted that democracy has within itself the seed of its
own destruction and that educators will impact this problem as well as be
impacted by it.

Outside the field of adult educators, there were many others who were
conducting research regarding the effectiveness of participative group decision making and democracy. In what was to become perhaps the most influ-
ential research since the Hawthorne studies, Lester Coch and John French
published the results in 1948 of a controlled experiment at the Harwood
Manufacturing sewing plant in Virginia. Although the plant had a reputation as a progressive industry, which provided health services, music,
recreation programs, and even plantwide votes on some issues, Harwood
was experiencing difficulties with workers adjusting to necessary changes
in work routines. Productivity would decrease, and some experienced workers would become frustrated and quit after each change was introduced.

Coch and French designed a controlled experiment involving four
groups. One group would have no participation in decision making regarding the changes. A second group would have elected representatives participate in the decision-making process. Two groups would have total participation in decision making regarding their changes.

The experiment showed that efficiency ratings after the change were
significantly better in the total participation groups and in the representative group than in the nonparticipatory group. Efficiency ratings were
quicker to increase after change in the total participation groups compared
with the representative group.

The nonparticipatory group experienced 17 percent loss of its workforce and numerous expressions of hostility toward supervision. The representative group had no loss and only one hostile act against supervision. The total participation group had no losses and worked well with supervision. Coch and French summarized their research findings in this way: "It is possible for management to modify greatly or to remove completely group resistance to changes in methods of work and the ensuing piece rates. This change can be accomplished by the use of Group meetings in which management effectively communicates the need for change and stimulates group participation in planning the changes." This study by Coch and French became concrete evidence in favor of creating a more participative workplace and was widely quoted for over thirty years.

THE 1950S

As Chapter 10 will cover, the late 1940s were a turbulent time of change for American industry. At the end of the war, union and management leaders were stating their desire to continue to work together in a cooperative manner. However, this broke down, and many of the adult educators who were involved in workplace democracy began to focus in other areas, such as literacy, and civil rights.

Many adult educators branched out in the 1950s, joining with social scientists to work in what is broadly referred to as the "human relations" movement in management theory. The establishment of the National Training Laboratory in Maine is a good example of how adult educators and others developed new approaches to address the lack of scientific methodology that Lindeman had identified.

In the postwar era of World War II, there can be little doubt that most managers and industrialists abandoned the concept of industrial democracy for many years. With a few notable exceptions, the 1950s and 1960s became the "age of autocracy" in American industry. While the Japanese and the Europeans began to build on the cooperative methods that won the war, American managers embarked on a crusade for control of their domain.

Perhaps the essence of autocratic opinion was best expressed by Robert McMurray in his popular 1958 article in the *Harvard Business Review*. McMurray doubted that managers would be willing to change their leadership styles to become more participative. A democratic approach requires commitment from leaders who rose to their positions through "no-quarter in-fighting" and who are determined to "keep the power in their own hands." At best, McMurray believed the managers may give lip service to democracy, but would maintain their authoritarian behaviors.

A second problem area for participation came from the need for uniformity of policies and practices and the perceived need for quick decisions in a competitive market economy, according to McMurray. And to these perceptions, McMurray offered a third problem of "bureaucratic traditions" of organizations that thrive on status and security. Middle management becomes composed of bureaucrats who "live by the book" and who perpetuate themselves.

McMurray argued that democratic group processes are flawed for several reasons:

1. Group decisions stimulate individual dependence on the group.
2. Some members fear to oppose the group.
3. When the group's members vary in status and power, subordinates are reluctant to disagree with their superiors.
4. Some group members become isolated from the group.

As an alternative to traditional autocracy and democracy, McMurray advocated a "benevolent autocracy." He accepted that management is by nature autocratic but argued that what is needed are "strong" autocrats who are not tyrants. McMurray asserted that most people want security and direction in their work and that the benevolent autocrat tells people what to do. McMurray saw the "benevolent autocrat" as a "father figure" who has power, prestige, and personal interest in his subordinates.

Leadership in the field of industrial democracy in the 1950s passed from the adult educators to social scientists, such as Rensis Likert, with the Institute for Social Research at the University of Michigan. Likert published a landmark study of the relationships between supervisory styles and productivity in the workplace in his 1961 work, *New Patterns of Management.*

Likert began this work by drawing from several research studies to show that whether you are looking at production workers, supervisors, or research scientists, in all cases, higher productivity is achieved when people have freedom in performing their work. When supervision provides freedom, then productivity, attendance, attitudes, and promotability of workers all improve.

Teamwork can have a positive effect on productivity, according to Likert. Several studies were used by Likert to illustrate that "work groups with greater pride in their capacity to produce or with greater loyalty and attraction to the group tend to be the groups producing at a higher level." Groups have great power in establishing standards of productivity, according to Likert, who reviewed the work of Coch and French, and subsequent studies by other social scientists.

The heart of Likert's book is the chapter dealing with an Institute for Social Research 1956 study conducted by Murse and Reimer of five hundred clerical employees in four parallel divisions in a large company. In two divisions, supervisory styles pushed decision making down into organizations, and the supervisors adopted "group methods of leadership." In the other two divisions, supervisory control was increased and decisions were moved up in the organization.

Both approaches provided an increase in productivity at about a comparable level in comparable divisions. However, in the divisions where supervisory control was increased, measured degrees of loyalty to the company fell, employees' "feeling of responsibility" dropped, turnover rates increased, and workers' attitudes toward supervisors fell. In the participative divisions, however, loyalty, attitudes, interests, and involvement in work all increased. People working in the participative system indicated increased satisfaction with all levels of management. Likert argued from this data that participative management will out-perform a hiearchical organization in the long term.

Overall, Likert observed that "low-producing managers feel that the way to motivate and direct behavior is to exercise control through authority." On the other hand, "widespread use of participation is one of the most important approaches employed by the high producing managers."

As Likert reviewed the controlled experiments, William Foote Whyte conducted research through field studies. In his 1961 publication, *Men At Work,* Whyte provided a snapshot of a wide range of organizational issues, including participation by workers. From a study conducted at Sears and Roebuck in the early 1950s, Whyte provided evidence related to organizational structures and patterns of supervision. Sears stores with fewer layers of management were found to have lower costs and higher profits. The managers in these stores with fewer layers of supervision were found to be more promotable to executive positions.

Whyte reported on a study of democratic approaches to management in which mechanics in a smelting operation participated in regular meetings and were encouraged to question and voice their ideas and to have input into promotional decisions. The participative approach led to improved morale and to successfully handling increasingly complex production demands.

A great deal of research concerning industrial democracy was conducted in Great Britain at the Tavistock Institute in the 1950s. Much of the Tavistock work grew out of the writings of Eric Trist regarding autonomous work groups in British coal mines. The Tavistock coal mining studies were conducted from 1954 to 1958, using the sociotechnical systems design process. To best match people's needs with the technology for mining, Trist and his design team, along with management and union leaders, agreed to form "self-regulating primary work groups" that oversaw their own production work. They found that this system enabled the supervisors to focus their attention in other areas. "The freedom needed higher up to manage change constructively is only won by establishing some freedom to manage at the bottom," Trist found.

P. G. Hurst compiled a technical follow-up on Trist's work, providing details in research methods and findings in his 1962 publication,

Autonomous Group Functioning. Hurst stated the operational conditions under which the Tavistock group found that autonomous teams can develop and thrive. First, the work task itself must be "itself autonomous, in the sense of being an independent and self-completing whole." Second, the work needs to be performed within an identifiable physical boundary, which provides "territory" the work group can "own." Another important point is that "control must be linked to variables that are observable and measurable." There must be effective ways for the workers to measure their own job output. Hurst's study provided a focus on the changes in the social structure that are needed to create a democratic work place.

THE 1960S

The management at the Harwood plant in Virginia, where Coch and French conducted their 1948 study, continued in their commitment to democratic management and to research. In the early 1960s, Harwood bought a competitor in the clothing business, Weldon Manufacturing, which had a traditional autocratic structure. Harwood management invited Alfred Marrow, David Bosers, and Stanley Seashore, from the University of Michigan, to document the change process at Weldon and to diagnose the successes and problems associated with the change process.

Data were collected from attitude surveys and economic indicators at Weldon before and after the changes to a more democratic management style, along with data from Harwood for the same time frame. The changes at Weldon included human relations training for supervisors, increased employee participation in decision making, reorganization along product lines, and improved training for operators. The economic indicators revealed a dramatic improvement at Weldon as a result of these changes. Productivity was able to increase to a point where Weldon could match Harwood's high productivity rates. Attitude survey data also indicated improvements in workers' perceptions about working at Weldon.

In one of the most prophetic writings of the 1960s, Paul Blumburg, a sociology professor at the City University of New York, cautioned people not to dismiss worker participation as an antiquated concept. Writing in his British publication, *Industrial Democracy: The Sociology of Participation*, Blumburg pointed out that there were major forces at work that would create a renewal in the issue of workplace democracy, noting that democratic self-determination was a major issue for university students in the 1960s.

Blumburg re-examined the Hawthorne Relay Assembly Room study and like Elton Mayo, Blumburg found that most accounts of the study missed a major component of the data. Blumburg assert that "a *major*, although not exclusive, explanation for the remarkable increases in productivity and morale lay in the crucial role which the test room workers played in determining the conditions under which they worked." As long as the researchers drew the operators into the decision-making process about physical and technical changes, productivity increased. Most accounts of Hawthorne only deal with this first two-year period of research. However, according to Blumburg, when the researchers later changed their methods and excluded the workers from discussion of the changes to be made, then the increases in productivity ended. Blumburg also provided an overview of the literature dealing with workplace participation, outlining work by Coch and French, Lewin, and Likert.

Other important research related to industrial democracy was continuing in Sweden in the 1960s with the Tavistock Institute, leading to Eric Rhenman's 1968 work, *Industrial Democracy and Industrial Management*. Rhenman observed that workers and managers might have very different definitions of industrial democracy that would keep them from working together. In essence, industrial democracy must be a way to satisfy two main objectives, according to Rhenman. These objectives are:

1. To establish a satisfactory balance between the various
   interests in the company.
2. To establish such working and management methods that
   the company's operation will lead to the desired result
   in the most efficient way.

The different stakeholders in a company such as the employees, management, local authorities, owners, customers, suppliers, and the state all have different interests that may conflict with each other, Rhenman noted. He defined stakeholders as "the individuals or groups which depend on the company for the realization of their personal goals and on whom the company is dependent." While management is itself a stakeholder, Rhenman observed that it is in the unique position to act as the mediator for the stakeholders.

Rhenman maintained that the first essential task for the organization, if it is to survive, is to achieve and maintain internal cooperation and then to create a continuous process for conflict resolution. As workers' interests are addressed, Rhenman believed that their representatives would gain access to better information

THE 1970S

Researchers in the United States and Great Britain continued to study the issue of autocracy and democracy in the workplace throughout the 1970s. In *Workplace Democratization: Its Internal Dynamics,* published in 1976, Paul Bernstein, a professor at the University of California, Irvine, conducted a comparative study of companies organized along democratic lines. Based on the examination of eighty-one sources that reported on thirty-one major democratization efforts, Bernstein established six components for workplace democracy Bernstein suggested using the term "democratization" to emphasize the point that the process of creating workplace democracy is what is highlighted in his study, not the final product. "The emphasis on process," Bernstein noted, "helps to keep us aware of the fact that, in all probability, there is no fixed, single, or final state of workplace democracy."

Bernstein provided an overview of many of the comparative cases in his study. For example, he presented the history and structure of 18 plywood manufacturing plants in the Pacific Northwest, formed between 1921 and 1955, which are owned by the employees.

In a similar approach, Daniel Zwerdling published *Workplace Democracy,* a 1978 review of a variety of workplace democracy programs that were discussed at the Third International Conference on Self-Management in 1976. The 1970s, according to Zwerdling, began a time when more people from research perspectives began to focus on the workplace as an area of study and began moving toward an implementation of democracy in the work setting. Zwerdling's review of cases included the work team systems at the General Foods plant in Topeka, Kansas, that utilized coaches instead of supervisors. Although the workers and plant management viewed the whole system as a success, corporate headquarters pushed the plant back into a hierarchical management style.

In the mining industry, Zwerdling reported on a two-year-old United Mine Workers Union and mine management joint effort at the Rushton Coal Mine in Pennsylvania. The project failed, according to Zwerdling, because of management resistance and slow expansion of the process to the whole mine. Zwerdling also reported on democratic management efforts at the Vermont Asbestos Group, the Mohawk Valley Community Corporation, the South Bend Lathe Company, Saratoga Knitting Mill, and at American University. Zwerdling provided an informative chapter on labor leaders' views on industrial democracy as well.

The use of sociotechnical systems design at the Tavistock Institute for twenty years was reviewed in 1972 by Peter Clark in his book, *Organizational Design.* According to Clark, the design process should focus on both technical and social structures, establishing both the work flow boundaries and the people boundaries. "Thus features of the technology and the existing customs and traditions have to be accounted for in the process of selecting from the alternative designs." The process for creating the design, according to Clark, should be one of joint investigation by a team that brings a diversity of perspectives to the study.

Paul Bate and Iain Mangham published the results of a five-year study in 1981 in their book, *Exploring Participation.* Bate and Mangham worked with one company as it transitioned from a traditional nonparticipatory organization into a participative workplace. From this study, they noted that "participation to managers, workforce, and ourselves remains a shapeless term, a process which is evolving slowly into something recognizably different from a state of non-participation, but as yet not tightly defined in and of itself."

Industrial democracy studies also continued in the 1970s in the Scandinavian countries, most notably in Norway and Sweden. Fred Emery, a professor at Australian National University, and Einar Thorsrud, a social psychology professor at the University of Oslo, began working on creating democratic structures in four Norwegian companies in the 1960s. Emery and Thorsrud served as researchers and consultants in efforts to enhance conditions for personal participation by workers in Norway. This work was carried out under a joint research committee consisting of members of the Trade Union Council, the Employers' Association, and the Norwegian federal government. The results of their studies were published in *Democracy at Work* in 1976. Their work placed an emphasis on involving the workers and managers in formulating the goals for the project and obtaining their agreement "on conditions to be changed and the criteria to be used in evaluating the outcome of whatever changes might be achieved."

For widespread implementation of industrial democracy, as in Norway, Emery and Thorsrud suggest this strategy. First, establish a joint union-management committee. Then choose experimental companies and analyze each for experimental sites. Establish worker-management action committees and develop a plan for change. The company needs to redefine policies to legitimize the changes, then institutionalize the changes and institutionalize the learning. Finally, information about results should be diffused to other sites.

Although many social scientists in the academic community were pursuing research that supported a transition into industrial democracy, researchers in the business schools tended to seek out ways to buttress the concept of the benevolent autocrat. Victor Vroom, the Chairman of the Department of Administrative Services at Yale University, investigated the decision making style of managers in an article entitled "Can Leaders Learn to Lead?" Vroom found that the autocratic model is more time-efficient, while the consultative and group decision-making styles improve the quality and acceptance of the decisions. Vroom noted, "there are also grounds for believing that participation contributes to individual and team development, and is likely to result in more informed and responsible behavior by subordinates in the future."

However, Vroom did not endorse the democratic style of decision making. He proposed that the ideal leader would vary his decision-making style based on his perception of the situational variables. Vroom offered no comment regarding the impact of these leadership style variations on the people working for the manager.

Writing to an audience of supervisors, Robert Keppler penned an article called "What the Supervisor Should Know about Participative Management" in 1978. Keppler suggested that increasing participation may be a good company tactic to defeat unions' organization efforts and that participative management can enhance the effectiveness of management's decision-making process. Participative management, according to Keppler, need not detract from management's prerogatives, but means taking the time to listen to the employees, confirming the observations made by others that the terms regarding participation and democracy can mean very different things to different people.

Barry Stein and Rosabeth Moss Kanter offered an alternative between autocratic and democratic management in a 1980 article entitled "Building the Parallel Organization." Stein and Kanter's parallel organization does not replace the autocratic structure, but supplements it by creating participative ad hoc teams to function alongside the conventional line organizations.

Kanter and Stein implemented an ad hoc project team approach at a nonunion manufacturer of electronic equipment. They created pilot groups that independently focused on organizational problems and then presented results that "astonished" the autocratic managers. Within the project teams, the authors observed a high degree of participation in problem solving and decision making by people who were normally excluded from decision making because of the autocratic structure.

THE 1980S

Research in the broad field of industrial democracy continued to spread in the 1980s as business schools, social scientists, organizational development consultants, and line managers initiated numerous studies and hundreds of companies began forming teams to support their quality improvement processes. New terms, such as empowerment, crept into the workplace vocabulary from social scientists, taking on new and diluted meanings. The 1980s also saw the reemergence of an active focus on industrial democracy issues among adult educators who often had personal ties with the industrial democracy activists of the 1930s and 1940s.

Liz Chell, a professor of organizational development, and Derrick Fielden, a professor of adult education, teamed together in the early 1980s to illustrate the essential linkage between adult education (which they refer to in British terms as non-formal education) and creating industrial democracy in the workplace. Rapid changes in technology are creating major stress in society and the workplace, according to Chell and Fielden. In an article entitled "Achieving Industrial Democracy via Non-Formal Education," they propose that two interrelated mechanisms that will help people cope with the stress of technical change are industrial democracy and adult education. Industrial democracy should consist of both direct involvement at the work level and representation at the board level of companies, according to Chell and Fielden, and at both levels people need to learn new skills for effectively contributing to the workforce.

Managers and workers often adopt certain myths regarding workers and education, according to Chell and Fielden. Some of these are the beliefs that shop floor workers have no desire to further education and that education means going back to school. In addition, there appears to be little time devoted to education in many businesses and paid education leave is not a reality in many countries, although it is common in Sweden, France, and Germany.

The role of education and industrial democracy was also considered by Robert Turner and Roger Count in their 1981 article, "Education and Industrial Democracy." Turner and Count conducted an action research project with British Trade Union members to define educational needs to further democratize industries. There are two broad areas of educational need for creating democracy in the workplace, according to Turner and Count. One need is to teach participative decision-making techniques to workers. The second need is to understand economic, industrial, and social facts and perspectives that will influence how boardroom decisions are made.

Turner and Count documented a televised and postal-based study program (distance learning) for trade union members in Britain that focused on teaching democratic principles and methods for participation. The project was a major step away from traditional adult education programs directed toward workers and designed to enable workers to be promoted into managerial positions. Instead, these programs focused on learning to apply democratic values as workers. Participants in this televised program reported numerous improvements in understanding industrial issues ranging from job satisfaction to government intervention in the economy. Participants gained a broader view of issues related to economic democracy, according to Turner and Count.

In the United States, many documented and undocumented experiments in industrial democracy were conducted in the 1980s, and are too numerous to cover in this chapter. In the specific area of adult education and industrial democracy, Frank Adams, Gary Hansen, and Martin Carnoy stand out for their contributions.

Adams reviewed the issue of educational needs within worker-owned cooperatives in a 1987 article, "Notes On an Emerging Pedagogy." Adams asked if the learning methods in practice are really suitable for a workplace based on democratic principles. With a belief that democratic principles are best grasped through direct participation, Adams advocated "nonformal learning" as one effective way to teach workers. This approach involves study circles or workshops. Working with the Industrial Cooperative Association, Adams and other staff members developed materials that would be "vital to any firm, then tailors them to the unique requirements of the labour-owned enterprise at each site."

Citing the Mondragon worker-owned project in Spain, Adams observed that "worker ownership will democratize knowledge," and noted that "the artificial barriers as to who gets to learn what must fall aside if cooperation is to flourish as the organizing medium for production."

Adams contrasted the fundamental assumptions of education in an investor-owned setting with education in a worker-owned setting. He observed that "no modern social movement which has wrought fundamental social change has been without some sort of self-elaborated, independent educational effort." Adams went on to state that "learning how to make decisions, to know, to value, and to gather and sort information becomes essential. Also, it means dynamic social change."

Adams had the opportunity to work with one of the great leaders in adult education, Myles Horton, who was a major contributor to labor education in the 1940s and the civil rights movement in the 1950s and 1960s. Adams' work is a primary example of the continuity of adult education processes being applied to a wide variety of settings in order to create change. After working with Horton, Adams teamed up with Gary Hansen to write *Putting Democracy to Work* in 1987, which addresses a broad range of issues concerning teaching employees in worker-owned cooperatives how to manage their own business. Adams and Hansen suggested that "the specific characteristics of such an educational plan will vary from firm to firm, but, in general will include vocational, performance, political, and cultural elements."

Adams and Hansen advocated conducting an educational needs assessment based on the beliefs that the opportunity for education should be open equally to all members of the organization. They suggest that "learning occurs through work itself, from informal dialogue, or formally through organized activities," and that everyone in the organization shares in a responsibility to be involved in shaping the organization's educational policies and program. The goal of this education, according to Adams and Hansen, is "to increase the abilities and skills of all members to control corporate decisions, resources, policies, and results."

On the other side of the continent, Martin Carnoy, at Stanford University, argued that formal and informal education in America "act in opposition to the cooperative and collective consciousness relevant to industrial democracy." In his article, "Education, Industrial Democracy, and the State," Carnoy reviewed the implications of the work of the Italian social theorist, Antonio Gramsci. Gramsci saw that the educational processes in any nation are based on the values of whatever group guides the nation. The social structures of a nation, such as its educational system, are shaped in order to continue the values of this leading group. If the leadership group in a nation or society wishes to conduct its industry in an autocratic manner, then democratic decision making skills will not appear in the school curriculum, since this would be incongruent with the goals of the dominant group. Therefore, Carnoy observed that worker-owned companies will need to create their own new form of education, consistent with the observations of Adams and Hansen.

THE 1990S AND BEYOND

Gramsci and Carnoy's observations, along with those of Adams and Hansen, can be expanded to the point where it is clear that the educational systems of industrialized nations and emerging democracies must be redesigned to emphasize democratic decision making, if industrial democracy is to continue to grow in response to the changes occurring within our societies.

The need for industrial democracy, and the diverse pathways for implementing democratizing practices, has moved empowerment and democracy beyond the boundaries of any single academic discipline. Diverse research, using a variety of research methods from many disciplines, can now be synthesized to clearly establish the benefits of industrial democracy and the variety of methods that can be employed to achieve this goal, even if the goal itself is a more of a process rather than a product.

The 1990s have already witnessed an explosion of academic research and popular publications that have shared new knowledge and experience about the uses of teams in the workplace, and the dynamics of empowerment. While the terminology like democratization seldom appears in this literature, the experiences, case studies, and theory of democratic governance and consentaneous decision making continue to grow.

Many business schools have now embraced the issue of participatory leadership and are integrating democratic concepts into management courses. Executive development courses taught by major universities now routinely teach democratic concepts to enable companies to achieve world-class competitive positions.

10

Unions, Adult Education, and Industrial Democracy

> The workers of America will continue to agitate, educate, and organize into trade unions and through their trade unions fight their own battles for industrial freedom, industrial justice, and industrial democracy."
> —Samuel Gompers, *Labor and the Employer*

There was a time when unions were a vital force committed to the creation of democracy in the workplace. When unions were still struggling for the right to exist within most companies, there was a strong desire among union leaders to create a workplace where democratic principles would be an important part of how the work environment was governed, as well as how the unions themselves would function.

THE EARLY YEARS

By the close of the First World War, the United States was in a high state of excitement and commitment to industrial democracy. One writer from this era, Jett Lauck, who had been secretary of the National War Production Board, captured the excitement in his book, *Political and Industrial Democracy: 1776-1926*. Lauck described industrial democracy as full employment; full protection against sickness, accident, and old age; minimum wage; maximum wage; profit sharing; abolition of absentee control; workers' control; and workers' ownership. Lauck pointed out that having made the world safe for democracy, it was now time to bring democracy to the workplace.

Many political leaders were supportive of industrial democracy, according to Lauck, especially President Woodrow Wilson. In an address by Wilson to the Congress in 1919, Wilson stated his perspective. "The object of all reform in this essential matter must be the genuine democratization of industry based upon a full recognition of those who work, in whatever rank, to participate in some organic way in every decision which directly affects their welfare."

There was support for industrial democracy from both the ranks of management and the unions. Lauck provided a 1919 labor statement that proclaimed, "There can not be a full release of productive energy under autocratic control of industry. There must be a spirit of cooperation and mutuality between employers and workers." Lauck also recorded the opinions of Edward Filene, president of a major retail store, who called for an industrial democracy "in which the employee has not only an adequate voice in the management and determination and control of work conditions, and an adequate stake in the results of work, but also, in addition, some guaranty that the management of the business shall be responsible and largely dependent for its rewards on its efficiency."

One well-documented example of an attempt toward industrial democracy was the Minnequa Steel Foundry in Pueblo, Colorado, a part of the Colorado Fuel and Iron Company, owned by John D. Rockefeller. The Minnequa program was studied by Ben Selekman in his work, *Employes' Representation In Steel Works,* under a grant from the Russell Sage Foundation. Minnequa's management initiated an employee representation plan in 1916 to achieve "more effective cooperation" with the workers. Under the plan, workers in eleven foundry divisions elected representatives, formed joint employee-management councils, and had joint conferences of all representatives and managers. The plan was voted on and approved by the workers, many of whom were members of small local unions, although there was no formal union-management relationship and no bargained contract.

Selekman noted that although management made few obligations to take issues to the work councils for approval, the workers were free to raise any issue they wished. Minnequa's joint committees were responsible, according to Selekman, for the foundry leading the country in creating an actual eight hour work day in 1918.

Involvement of the workers also led to other changes observed by Selekman. Safety was improved because of many employee suggestions, sanitary conditions were greatly improved (which was an important point during the fatal influenza epidemics of those years), and medical facilities were also improved. The joint committees were also used for reviewing wages. Employee representatives toured steel mills in Illinois, Indiana, Ohio, and Pennsylvania and were involved in setting wage rates. During one period of downturn, the employees decided on a 15 percent pay cut to stay competitive.

Despite broad support, the move for industrial democracy faltered over the role that unions would play in the workplace. Lauck credited a group of "reactionary employers" with being opposed to unions and creating "the alleged open-shop movement." At Minnequa, for example, steel workers supported the American Federation of Labor's national steel strike in 1919. After the strike failed, returning workers had to sign an "open-shop" pledge.

Samuel Gompers, the leader of the American Federation of Labor, considered industrial democracy to be the ultimate goal of the labor movement. However, he resisted any efforts towards democratization which did not follow the path of formation of a union first. In his 1920 book, *Labor and the Employer*, Gompers stated that "Industrial democracy is the great goal of the future." Gompers said, "It is the thing to which the eyes of men are turned. It must and will be a real democracy of industry. No sham will do." Gompers observed, "There is a growing consciousness of the determination on the part of the workers to put an end to all that savors of industrial autocracy. With this object in view, the workers of America will continue to agitate, educate, and organize into trade unions and through their trade unions fight their own battles for industrial freedom, industrial justice, and industrial democracy."

Samuel Gompers clearly believed that true democracy in the workplace could only be achieved where workers were organized into trade unions that would have the union as a national spokesman for the workers. He rejected any forms of participation that did not start with the creation of a trade union for the workforce. In his last speech to the American Federation of Labor in 1924, Gompers stated that "the only influence of power which challenges this employer's autocracy and dictatorship is the American labor movement of our country, and all other democratic industrial countries."

Gompers' right arm in the American Federation of Labor, William Walling, maintained that "organized labor works for the constant extension of this beginning of democratic government in industry." According to Walling, democracy in industry would consist of collective bargaining coupled with a voice in the management of business.

Other labor leaders were also supportive of the concept of industrial democracy, although they may have differed from Gompers on how it could be achieved. Huey Long and Constance Lawry have chronicled the efforts of Fannia Mary Cohn, of the International Ladies Garment Workers Union, who worked in the 1920s on establishing workers' education programs for her union and for the American Federation of Labor. The major purpose of organizing workers' education, according to Cohn, was to train "a small minority to lead their fellows to a land of industrial democracy."

THE 1930S

The struggle for the existence of unions was a violent and emotional effort throughout the 1930s. As the Roosevelt administration's new laws regarding labor relations began to come into existence, the ability to unionize became somewhat easier. By the beginning of the Second World War, the organization of unions was picking up great speed.

Much of the interest in democracy within organized labor in the 1930s focused on building democracy within the unions, not on industrial democracy. The main vehicle for this development was found in the worker education movement, led by the American Labor Education Service.

In an article in the 1936 edition of *The Journal of Adult Education,* Eleanor Coit, the Director of the American Labor Education Service discussed workers' education activities created through the Federal Emergency Relief Administration. Coit's interest lay in building this temporary worker education link with the federal government into an ongoing permanent relationship. She provided comparisons with state-sponsored workers' education programs in Denmark and Sweden. Coit noted how workers' education had progressed in Scandinavia by government funding through grants to local autonomous adult education programs, in contrast to the American practice of government funds being spent by government agencies.

Coit found that Swedish and Danish adult education programs provided classes in economics and history, but had moved well beyond the traditional classroom plan. "Wide use of the short institute on special problems, as well as organized study by political groups, gives background for programs of action," Coit observed. While lecture was commonly used in classes, Coit found that "considerable experimentation in nonauthoritarian methods of teaching is now being carried on."

During the 1930s, the business community remained divided on the issue of industrial democracy. Some industrialists, such as Paul Litchfield (Goodyear Tire and Rubber Company) were outspoken opponents of any involvement of workers in decision making. They were joined by the National Association of Manufacturers and the U.S. Chamber of Commerce. Some industry leaders, such as Owen Young, of General Electric, were still supportive of efforts to increase participation of workers in decision making.

THE 1940S

The war years saw an amazing era of union and management cooperation which had not existed since the end of the First World War. At the request of President Roosevelt, management in defense plants along with their union leaders created five thousand labor-management committees to help increase war production. Dorothea de Schweinitz, a manager in the War Production Board, chronicled the era shortly after the war in her book, *Labor and Management in a Common Enterprise.*

Of these five thousand committees, de Schweinitz estimated that one-half were only involved in selling war bonds, conducting rallies, and conducting blood drives. They had no impact on decision making at work. However, some two thousand committees operated suggestion systems and worked on safety issues and lowered absenteeism. De Schweinitz estimated that about five hundred were very active in enhancing "production methods, improving quality of work, conservation of materials, care of tools, and equipment, and discussion of production schedules."

De Schweinitz provided many specific examples of the results of labor and management cooperation through work councils. Workers producing insecticide for use in the tropics surpassed management's goal of 600 units a day, and through worker-initiated improvements, achieved a 24,000 per day production level. Reduction of scrap, better care of tools, and many specific quality improvements and improvements in training are cited. According to de Schweinitz, workers provided over 1.5 million documented suggestions for improvements through the joint committees. Suggestions at one shipyard alone saved over 700,000 man-hours in production time.

At the close of the war, most industries indicated they would continue the joint labor-management committees, according to de Schweinitz. There is evidence of union and management cooperation continuing in some areas up to 1950. For example, William Foote Whyte, a professor of Industrial Relations at Cornell, documented a dynamic change at Inland Steel Container Company in Chicago in his book, *Patterns for Industrial Peace.* After two decades of bitter struggle, management and the unions at Inland were establishing a new cooperative environment. The company was able to evolve from management practices in the 1930s, which Whyte describes as a dictatorship based on terrorism. In response to management's autocratic actions, the workers organized a union under the Congress of Industrial Organizations. Bad relations between union leadership and management peaked in 1946 with a 191-day strike.

Whyte's study focused on the specific negotiation of a new contract in 1947. Providing a detailed account of the negotiating process, including many verbatim descriptions of the dialogue, Whyte showed how a gradual pattern of understanding between the adversaries was achieved. In summarizing activities since the new contract, Whyte made this observation: "In the years 1948 to 1950, we see two interrelated trends. An increasing area of activity is being handled *jointly* by union and management officers working together. And more and more people in both organizations are becoming actively involved in the cooperation process."

However, by 1949, Dorothea de Schweinitz had found that most joint union and management cooperative efforts from the war years were over and that a new era was dawning that was hostile towards industrial democracy. In 1949, de Schweinitz reported that "National union officers, though in favor of union-management cooperation on production, generally write off the war committees as a bed debt in which their members made concessions but did not gain acceptance for many of their ideas for improving production. They consider that the discontinuance of the vast majority of committees at the close of the war is evidence that employers ask for cooperation from the union only when they need it, not as a permanent basis of operation."

CHANGING DIRECTIONS

It turned out that 1949 was a year of major change for the American labor movement. In part because of the failure of companies to follow through with the cooperation from the war years, and in part due to the "red scare" sweeping the country as part of Senator Joseph McCarthy's hearings, the major American unions moved away from their commitment to industrial democracy. Concepts that had been endorsed by President Wilson and many business leaders were tainted as being leftist. The unions decided to hold on to the gains they had achieved, adopting a status quo position that did not push further for industrial democracy in the face of McCarthyism.

When the unions abandoned their commitment to the pursuit of industrial democracy, they also abandoned the union organizers and educators who had been the passionate life force of the union movement. Union educators, like Myles Horton, who had created the nation's most successful school for training union organizers, left the labor movement and began focusing their efforts on other progressive efforts, such as the struggle to end racial segregation. From that point on, the American union movement began a slow decline in both spirit and membership, which has continued to the last years of the century.

Even worse, some unions not only abandoned their commitment to industrial democracy, they also abandoned their commitment to democratic governance within the union itself. Unionism lost credit with a large part of the "Baby Boom" generation in the 1960s since the unions aligned themselves politically with conservative political leaders, and remained unwilling to allow democracy to flourish within their organizations.

The strategies pursued by unions in the United States met the short-term needs of their members, but sacrificed the long-term interests of the workers. The decision to maintain a status quo that centered around adversarial relationships contributed to the decline of trade unionism by fostering unnecessary conflict that alienated the public. A great deal of energy was devoted to unsuccessful attempts to rewrite the labor laws to give unions more power, creating an unrealized hope that by changing the rules, the unions could achieve their objectives. However, throughout the 1960s and 1970s, specific unions continued to engage in cooperative efforts with enlightened managers, keeping alive the possibility of a broader standard of cooperation.

Fledgling efforts concerning quality of working life in the 1970s grew into major total quality management efforts by the late 1980s. The emphasis on employee participation in teams from the quality gurus forced management and union leaders alike to take tentative steps back onto common ground in many organizations. Decades of distrust were being overcome as management and union teams began to work together again to keep factories open and improve productivity in the face of foreign competition.

These initial efforts to work together to improve productivity have had a positive influence on labor and management relations, according to University of Wisconsin economist, Dale Belman. Belman published the results of his study of the effects of joint labor and management programs in a chapter entitled "Unions, the Quality of Labor Relations, and Firm Performance" in *Unions and Economic Competitiveness* published by the Economic Policy Institute. Belman pointed out, "By raising the level of trust in the workplace, they (teams) provide a foundation for a cooperative approach to differences and conflicts."

OPPORTUNITIES FOR DEMOCRACY

In working within a unionized environment, the change agent must address specific conditions to achieve collaboration. The three greatest challenges involve (1) helping management accept the right of the union to exist, (2) helping the union accept the need for a balance of power for the good of the organization, and (3) helping both sides understand that the other side is made up of factions, not a monolithic mass of opinion.

Enlightened managers recognize that unions can provide stability and predictability within a work place. The unions can provide a healthy check and balance and can help ensure that employees are involved in the decision-making process so that they are committed to the goals of the organization. Economists, such as Dale Belman, have reviewed numerous studies of the impact of unions on productivity. Belman has noted that "contrary to the fears of neoclassical economists, unions do not of themselves lower productivity. The majority of studies find that unions are associated with higher productivity. Of those which have not found positive effects, there is typically either no effect or a negative effect associated with a poor labor relations climate."

Less enlightened managers see the union only as an obstacle that they must work around to get things done. Of course, there are unions that have indeed become obstacles to their companies, but that is usually the result of a long history of actions initiated by management that have created a climate of distrust.

Union leaders must accept the fact that an organization needs an executive function, balanced by a representative function. The union represents the interests of its constituents, who are important stakeholders in the organization. However, every union leader, along with every member of a union, must become aware of the economic reality known as the "Tragedy of the Commons," which was observed in colonial America. Given the opportunity to graze their cows on the common land, villagers would tend to overgraze and destroy the commons before putting their cows on their own land. In other words, people may take actions for their individual short-term good which are detrimental to their collective long-term good. For this reason, effective democracy requires an executive function that is willing to make unpopular decisions. Union leaders must respect the humanity of managers when tough decisions must be made, as sometimes happens in a market economy.

The final difficulty is in getting union leaders and managers to recognize that "the other side" is not a solid mass of like-minded people, but usually consists of people with a range of opinions on various issues. There will be a range of opinions among the unions' members and there will be a range of opinions among the management ranks. Labor peace and cooperation is just like peace and cooperation between two conflicting nations. Each nation has different factions that vie for power. When the nations' dominant factions are bent on conflict, there will be war. When the nations' dominant factions are bent on cooperation, there will be peace. The same holds true with labor and management. Labor and management leaders who seek cooperation must help one another "win" within their own constituencies.

In a unionized environment, the change agent must find leaders on both sides who want cooperation and help them achieve peace. This means listening to what each side needs to have from the other to convince their constituents that cooperation is in everyone's interest. In most cases it means that management must be the first to hold out the olive branch.

ESTABLISHING THE GROUND RULES

A set of guidelines for cooperative activities should be developed, requiring many iterations to hammer out a set of principles acceptable to both leaderships. The guidelines must clearly state that management will not use the union's cooperation as a means of bypassing the union or seeking to eliminate the union. The slightest sign that management would like to do away with the union will naturally lead the union members to choose a new leader who will fight to protect the members' interests.

The guidelines should establish a joint union and management steering committee to drive to cooperative process. The committee should be jointly chaired by the top representatives of management and the union(s) at the specific facility. The steering committee should consider all proposals for joint union and management team efforts and should review progress reports from these teams in a timely manner. If management or the union does not want to participate jointly in a proposed activity, then their leadership should have the right to veto the proposed project. Management should have the right to carry forth a vetoed project, with the clear understanding that it is not part of the joint effort.

When proposals for new activities are brought before the joint union and management steering committee, there should be time for discussion, but neither side should be asked to commit immediately to the proposal. Both sides should have twenty-four hours to caucus and discuss the idea, and then communicate back to each other. This allows each side to have the full opportunity to review the merits of a proposal in some degree of privacy.

The steering committee should also be the forum for raising concerns as to how both sides are adhering to the agreement. It is very common for some supervisors and some union members to resist the collaborative effort, seeking to undermine it so that they can return to the familiar confrontational patterns of the past. Each side should be willing to point out these problems as they arise with the expectation that these concerns will be quickly corrected.

Companies should look seriously at paying for full-time union staff members to work on facilitating team efforts and to serve as trainers to enable the workforce to participate in problem solving and decision making efforts. Full time union staff people to support other efforts, such as safety, are also a good investment in a collaborative setting.

As part of the guidelines, an honest effort must be made to create a "level playing field" by involving the union's members in decision-making efforts. To invite one union person to participate in a team where all the other members are "company" people, will be asking the union member to play on an uneven field. Joint union and management teams should be cochaired by union and management representatives and should try to have a balanced number of participants.

When it comes to selecting which bargaining unit people will participate on a specific team effort, the selection decision should be left up to the union leadership, with the understanding that positive minded, and technically competent people will be chosen. Bargaining unit leaders are understandably concerned when management attempts to hand-pick the hourly people they want to serve on a team.

Both union and management need to be committed to ensuring that pressure is not brought to bear on employees for participating in a collaborative effort. The union leadership needs to make sure that its members do not harass those who are willing to work with management. Likewise, the company needs to ensure that employees are allowed to fully participate when they have been selected to serve on a team.

If an organization in a unionized setting wants to move toward empowered work teams, or self-managed teams, the union leadership needs to be involved in the process. To have a successful transition, union staff people can help in training the workers to be involved in self management and can help ensure that adequate boundaries are defined and performance indicators are in place to assist the empowered team.

The union will also play a vital role in helping to ensure that employees who take on a greater set of responsibility through work in empowered teams are recognized and/or rewarded. The union can help assure that support processes, such as compensation, reinforce a collaborative team effort through practices such as gainsharing.

A joint union and management committee can also be established to provide recognition for teams and individuals. These joint committees have much greater credibility that management-only teams, since the recognition is agreed to by peers as being truly deserving. Joint union and management committees are often more demanding in giving awards and recognition, ensuring that only the truly deserving groups are recognized.

Any joint union and management effort must be based on an agreement that no bargaining unit people will be laid off as a result of any ideas or efforts coming out of the joint teams or committees. If this agreement cannot be reached as a foundation for the effort, no reasonable union leader will be able to work in partnership with the company.

MAINTAINING A SYSTEMS PERSPECTIVE

Perhaps the most important point for the change agent or the empowerment planning team to remember in working with a joint union-management effort is the systems view of the organization. The union is a major subsystem in an organization. Union and management relations are influenced by actions which involve senior management, middle management, and the front line supervisor. The union provides a feedback loop to senior management about situations occurring out in the organization between front-line supervision and employees. Union leaders must remember that they are a subsystem, not the whole system. There are other stakeholders whose needs must also be addressed and met by the organization.

There are many possible approaches for joint union and management collaboration that will lead to various degrees of empowerment and democracy. Organizations can start small with joint union and management councils and project teams. They can work together to overhaul their methods for bargaining and complaint resolution. Organizations can involve union and management leadership together in strategic planning, and can certainly provide positions for union members on governing bodies as full voting members to represent employee interests.

APPENDIX:
Opportunities for Praxis

1. What are the perceptions among the mangers in your organization toward unions? How can those perceptions be challenged?

2. If your organization has a union, how can the union contribute to the democratization effort in your organization? What hurdles must be overcome in management and in the union?

3. What are four actions that your organization could take over the next six months to improve joint union and management collaboration?

4. What are the four excuses that your managers and union leaders will raise that will prevent a collaborative effort? How can these excuses be overcome?

11

The Organizational Gardener

> My vision was clarified politically during the Depression when we were faced with capitalism coming apart. There was a socialist alternative and a fascist alternative, an authoritarian and a democratic alternative. I chose at that time, out of that experience and out of my religious ethical beliefs, to opt on the side of a democratic solution to the problems, not an authoritarian solution. That's frozen into a principle. I believe in democracy versus authoritarianism.
> —Myles Horton, *We Make the Road by Walking*

In this closing chapter there are several ideas that need to be explored in order for the organizational gardener to maintain a healthy perspective about his or her work. The first issue concerns the creation of an appropriate understanding of what it means to have a bountiful harvest in an organization. The second issue deals with the new opportunities that arise from successful gardening. Another issue for consideration involves the problems of burnout for gardeners and how this problem can be avoided.

BOUNTIFUL HARVESTS

It can be very impressive to have twenty rows of corn all come in at the same time. So much corn! So much success! But, a huge amount of a single crop is not what makes a bountiful harvest. The best harvest occurs when there is plenty of corn, along with okra, tomatoes, peppers, watermelons, and cantaloupes, all at once. Each is a small victory, which is enhanced by all the other simultaneous small victories.

The same is true for organizational gardening. There is usually not one single big success that makes an organization great. In fact, most organizations can point to one area of excellence that they have. It may be in quality or in succession planning, an awards program, or an innovative training plan. There is a tendency to expend a great amount of energy on a single showcase program while leaving other areas unattended. This is the organizational equivalent of growing twenty rows of corn, but having no other food to use for dinner.

An effective organizational garden needs balance and perspective. It requires many small victories that create an overall abundance rather than one or two showcase programs. The organizational gardener must encourage the organization to have the patience to carefully work on many issues over time. The end results will have a much greater impact for the organization when multiple efforts can be harvested together. For instance, a simultaneous focus on controlling costs and improving quality will have a much greater and healthier impact on an organization than either effort taken as a stand-alone program. A combined effort to develop an assessment process, career planning, mentoring, and cultural diversity will have a much greater impact on an organization than any individual component given special emphasis.

Organizations that have attempted to implement Dr. W. Edwards Deming's Fourteen Obligations for Management have encountered this same fact. One cannot implement isolated principles from Deming's Fourteen Points. They must all be implemented, since they are mutually dependent. It is very difficult to point to a situation and state that "here is point number four" at work.

None of this will come as any surprise when we recall that organizations are systems that will react to change in a holistic and biological manner. Our brief overview of systems theory in Chapter 1 reminds us that the subsystems of an organization are mutually dependent, so that change to one part of the organization will impact and be influenced by the rest of the organization.

Many organizations tend to reserve their celebrations for the big victories that they can achieve. Perhaps it is the one millionth hour worked without an accident, or the ten thousandth car to roll off a production line. These are wonderful milestone events that should be celebrated. But since the most bountiful harvest comes about as the result of many small victories, there should be many small celebrations for the successes in an organization. An emphasis on seeing the successes and celebrating a success every week is one of the vital methods for creating the positive synergy needed in an organization for sustaining harvests over many years.

Most Americans have become too far removed from the source of their food to marvel at the amazing way in which a vegetable grows. Therefore, many no longer pause to give thanks for the meals they enjoy. We lump all our thanks into one weekend in November, which is usually an exercise in over-eating and watching football. We tend to extend this same behavior to the workplace, where we do not express thanks to each other for the daily and weekly successes we encounter. Then we lump our celebrations into a few parties that are excessive and even uncomfortable for the people who are supposed to be honored.

A few decades ago, successful gardening and farming required the use of a mule or a horse, which had to be tended in order to be able to sustain the garden. Every farmer knew that you had to feed your mule so you could plow your field. Today's farmers know that their tractors and combines have to been in good operating condition to be successful. Even for the backyard gardener, the roto-tiller and the hoe must be kept clean and sharp to be effective.

Organizational gardeners must have a similar concern regarding the protection and care for the tools in their organization that are necessary to create success. The most important resources are the people, whose ideas and energy are what makes an organization successful. The organization that places people secondary to buildings or production equipment or any other physical or financial resource will have great difficulties in achieving long term success.

The process of celebrating the harvest must have its attention and focus on the people who made the harvest happen. The celebration process needs to include all the people who contribute, both directly and indirectly, to a success.

SUCCESS CREATES NEW OPPORTUNITIES

The gardener stands on a hilltop and creates a vision for what the garden will look like. This visioning exercise is followed by long periods of hard work, creating a multitude of small victories, which, overall, add up to a bountiful garden. There may be long periods of work, building up the soil, working on the irrigation, planting and hoeing the weeds. Eventually, there is a bountiful harvest. Even in the time of harvest there is hard work to be done to sustain the harvest for as long as possible.

Occasionally a gardener may have a unique method for growing one crop especially well, and may be reluctant to share that knowledge with others, to remain special. However, most gardeners know that they can magnify the rewarding experience of gardening by sharing their skills and insights with others.

It is vitally important for the organizational gardener to serve as a schol-ar-practitioner, sharing the information he or she has gained from experience. American agriculture has grown to amazing levels of productivity because farmers, seed companies, researchers, and implement companies have been willing to pool their knowledge about how to be successful. In particular, the agriculturists have emphasized how to create success by integrating activities that are subsystems of a larger systems. On the small scale, it is like feeding your leftover corn stalks to your horses and using the manure to fertilize your garden next year.

Organizational gardeners need to share their successes with one another in a variety of ways. There has been a recent growth in publications that share success stories written by the people in the field who are creating these successes. This is an important activity for organizational gardeners to participate in by writing for these journals and by reading these journals. The important knowledge about what works in an organization is being created out in the organizations, not in the business schools. Most of the publications from the business schools are broad assessments of what is occurring, which also have important value. However, it is very important for the practitioners to take an active role in reporting their results and failures to their colleagues around the country.

Another way to amplify success in organizational gardening is through participation at conferences, either as a participant or as a presenter. Presentations at conferences can be enhanced when the gardener can place his or her report in the context of the work that has gone on over the preceding decades in the general areas of democratization, quality improvement, and organizational development. It is sometimes a little sad to hear someone reporting on a "new" success that has actually been around for a long time.

There is a need for a different style of conference to help create the knowledge base to democratize the workplace and to bring about the most effective systems for improving quality and human resources. Most conferences currently organize around a series of presentations that include a small time for questions and answers, with little time for dialogue and comparison.

The Highlander Research and Education Center in eastern Tennessee has pioneered an alternative style of learning conference over the past fifty years that has been effective in providing the educational base for the civil rights movement, rural literacy programs, and some of the more effective approaches to protecting the environment. People journey from all around the globe to experience a Highlander program, which engages people in dialogue to explore issues and create answers, rather than a one-way presentation about what one organization is doing. Many of my own thoughts about workplace democratization came about as the result of a Highlander session with the late Myles Horton and with Paulo Freire, in which educators spent a day discussing the impact of education on empowerment of people at work, in communities, and in creating social change.

A new form of conference, based on the Highlander model, is needed for organizational gardeners. Instead of meeting in major hotels and dressing up in our suits and dresses, we need to be gathering in a circle of rocking chairs and engaging one another in dialogue into the early morning hours. Instead of looking for the next Deming or Juran in the crowd, we need to recognize that we are all part of a movement that is going to succeed due to thousands of unheralded people. For every Rosa Parks and Martin Luther King, Jr. (who were both active at Highlander, by the way) there are going to be ten thousand people who create change in their own community and who are the real owners of the change process.

AVOIDING GARDENER BURNOUT

Years ago I watched rather helplessly as one of my gardening mentors burned himself out. I tried to advise him that the ground was too rocky to support the type of change he wanted to implement. No gardener ever worked harder, or was to my knowledge more dedicated to his organization. He was literally a prophet who would not be honored in his own village. A decade later, his ideas, which were seen as troublesome, have become accepted as great truths by his organization, and a few of his disciples still speak his name with reverence, but he is long gone. He worked so hard and developed so much stress that it aggravated a medical condition and forced him into an early retirement.

Everyone can burn out. Everyone can reach a point of despair when they decide there is just no hope for their organization. Remember that the best way to keep people from becoming empowered is to kill off those who would facilitate the empowerment process, whether that be through teaching people to read or teaching people in the workplace how to create change. Most organizational gardeners will either encounter a moment of despair or find a time when they are the target of those who wish to maintain the status quo.

The first step in avoiding burnout is to recognize that it really exists and that it is a highly probable occurrence for anyone who seeks to generate change in their organization. Consider W. Edwards Deming for a moment. By many accounts, Dr. Deming considered himself a failure before his final decade. He had devoted his life to teaching and building on the concepts of Walter Shewhart, and had had great success in Japan. But he was unable to reach the industries in his own country that could benefit from his knowledge. Deming must have surely had his days of depression, but ultimately he persevered, and when conditions became right, his message began to be received.

Each gardener is going to have days, weeks, or even years, when he or she labors like Deming, with no obvious impact. It is said by many that an idea has to be offered seven times before it is understood and accepted in an organization. Many of us are only working on the third or fourth attempt, so we probably have a long way to go before the message will be heard.

There are several methods to avoiding burnout that the organizational gardener can learn from the real gardener. First, I was impressed as a boy by my great-uncle, who would always admonish me to never put away a hoe or shovel without first cleaning it off. This devotion to keeping your tools clean and sharp is a vital aspect of effective gardening. Stephen Covey has captured this idea as one of his seven habits of effective people, which he calls sharpening your saw.

You can keep your hoe clean (or your saw sharp) by collaborating and through self-study. It is very important for the organizational gardener to occasionally take some time off to listen to what others are doing and to add new tools to the tool kit. Going to a conference or a professional society meeting is a vital method for staying fresh and avoiding burnout, if these sessions provide an opportunity to learn new ideas and compare notes.

Self-study offers an ongoing, and lower cost, method for keeping the organizational gardener's energy level up. The literature of the magazines for practitioners offers many good ideas. However, it is also beneficial to delve into the resources of a major library to see what new ideas you can uncover. There is a major literary source regarding the general field of organizational gardening that is published in other countries that most gardeners are not hearing about. Codetermination in Germany is an exciting topic. Worker cooperatives in India offer other ideas. Prior to the civil unrest in Yugoslavia, there were many promising studies related to work place democracy. It helps to cultivate an international perspective on this general field. Most gardeners can get a lot of energy by digging a bit more into the history of their movement. This book has only touched on some of the interesting work that has gone on before us.

Gardeners avoid stress by working in the morning and evening hours and avoiding the heat of the day. Organizational gardeners need to time their activities to the rhythms of their organization. An innovation can be rejected as irrelevant when introduced at the wrong time, and this can lead to major disappointment. Timing is critical, so bide your time and wait for the right opportunity. There's no sense in burning yourself out when the organization is not ready. Spend your time wisely in preparing the soil and wait for the right moment to step in with an energetic intervention.

Perhaps the most important method for avoiding burnout is to remember the joy in what you are doing. It is not easy to hoe a row of beans. But it helps to see the joy in your contribution to making beans possible. It is not easy to implement organizational change, but it helps to see the joy in emancipating people from systems that are inefficient and that create endullment.

The organizational gardener needs to recognize that his or her efforts are centered in the concept of emancipatory learning. Although there are many systems issues to address, such as performance appraisals and reward processes, the root issue involves the "conscientization" process, in which managers and employees all recognize that they share a common interest in creating the most democratic processes possible to maximize the efficiency and effectiveness of their organizations. The labor versus management problems that dominated many companies for decades are the result of the initial failures of the efforts to achieve workplace democracy in the Woodrow Wilson era. Our thinking processes have come to accept autocratic decision making, and the conflict associated with autocracy, as good, right, and normal. In spite of many significant research findings to the contrary, the autocracy has been maintained in most organizations. The fundamental task ahead is to generate a new awareness that a balance of perspectives and a balance of influence in decision making will allow organizations to reach their most successful level of quality, productivity, and compliance to the many rules and regulations that have been enacted to protect the environment, and the health and safety of workers. The best way to avoid burnout is for the organizational gardener to keep an eye on the long-term goal and to understand his or her place in the long historical process in which we participate on a daily basis.

CLOSING THOUGHTS

Chapter 1 offered the observation that organizations can best be described as systems, using an organic model rather than a mechanical model. Myles Horton, at the Highlander Center for Research and Education, made this point in a film that interwove footage of Highlander programs in civil rights, literacy, and environmental education with interviews with Horton as he worked in his garden, preparing the soil, sewing the seeds, hoeing weeds, and harvesting the crop.

In essence, all of us who labor in any type of organization, seeking to grow democratic processes, are organizational gardeners. We must begin our work by having the end in mind, bringing democracy into the workplace, based on the belief that democracy is the best form of government in any setting. With the end in mind, we can work the soil, plant the seeds, pull the weeds, nurture, and eventually see the harvest.

To be an organizational gardener requires much patience and perseverance. If this book shows anything at all, it is that the movement to achieve democracy in the workplace is a long, gradual process. Democracy can only be achieved one organization at a time. Each organizational gardener has a unique and special challenge in his or her "garden." Hopefully, the tools and processes in this book will serve as an effective gardener's manual that will be useful in many situations.

A few years ago, I was invited to write a scholarly critique of the work of Dr. W. Edwards Deming from the perspective of an adult educator. I concluded that while Dr. Deming had some flaws in his manner of teaching, his message was right on target. There is no instant pudding, as Deming used to say.

There are no easy miracle grow steps that will turn your benevolent autocrats into empowering leaders. Each organization will have its unique specific challenges that require diagnosis and different levels of effort. Some will find the labor easy and can receive public credit for the quality of their garden. Others will find themselves working with many problems, so their task will be more difficult, and they may labor for many years without any recognition.

Dr. Deming's message was not a complete package of knowledge for effective organizational gardening. No one has that package, and no single academic discipline contains all the necessary knowledge within its academic boundaries to bring about the democratization of the workplace. To be successful in creating workplace democracy, we need gardeners who come from many backgrounds and who will wield a wide assortment of tools.

The organizational gardener must blend the knowledge of many disciplines in order to effectively assess the status and needs of an organization and to apply the right actions to the specific conditions of his or her organizational setting. We can each learn from one another, and we can all learn from those who have gone before us, such as Mary Parker Follett, Moses Coady, Dorothy Hewitt, Kurt Lewin, Rensis Likert, W. Edwards Deming, Joseph Juran, Myles Horton, Paulo Freire, and many, many others.

There are many problems along the way. The soil must be worked and re-nourished over time. Much of the seed that is cast will fall on rocks and among thorns. Economic conditions can flood out a crop or leave it to bake in the sun. There are parasites that will feast on the crop as it grows, seeking their own interests. The harvest might be years away, so it is easy to lose focus and be diverted to work on side issues.

Most of all, there must be a sense of praxis. We must each enhance our understanding of theory by study, dialogue, and reflection on our theory based upon our observations from our practice. We must each improve our practice based upon the refinement of our understanding of the theory related to organizations, democracy, productivity, quality, and change.

The fundamental issue in today's workplace is the same as it was in 1916 when Henry Gantt wrote his book, *Industrial Leadership*. Gantt observed, "It is safe to say that it is only under a task system of management that the highest development can be reached, and it is our problem therefore to develop a task system on the basis of democracy that will yield as good, or better results than those now in operation under autocracy."

The underlying theme of the twentieth century has been the struggle for democracy, among the nations and among the people. Democracy at the national level, in local government, and in the workplace, will continue to be the major challenge for humanity in the twenty-first century.

We now have 90 years of experience and "lessons learned" upon which to draw. With the right vision, the right tools, and the right determination, organizational gardeners will assure that democracy blossoms and that harvests will enrich all the people.

Bibliography

Adams, Frank. *Unearthing Seeds of Fire.* Winston-Salem, N.C.: John F. Blair, 1975.

Adams, Frank. "Notes on an Emerging Pedagogy." *Education With Production* (June 1987): pp. 41-49.

Adams, Frank and Hansen, Gary. *Putting Democracy to Work.* Eugene, Ore.: Hulogos' Communications, Inc., 1987.

Adizes, Ichak. *Industrial Democracy: Yugoslav Style.* New York: Free Press, 1971.

Alitzer, Christopher C. "Four Steps to Empowerment." *Tapping the Network Journal* (Spring 1993) 21-23.

American Productivity Center. *Designing Effective Work Teams.* Houston, Tex.: American Productivity Center, 1986.

American Society for Training and Development. *National Report.* Alexandria, Va.: American Society for Training and Development, 1991.

Anton, Frank. *Worker Participation: Prescription for Industrial Change.* Calgary, Alberta: Deteselig Enterprises, 1980.

Aubrey, Chalres and Felkins, Patricia. *Teamwork: Involving People In Quality and Productivity Improvement.* Milwaukee, Wis.: Quality Press, 1988.

Auvine, Brian, et al. *A Manual for Group Facilitators.* Madison, Wis.: Center for Conflict Resolution, 1978.

Avery, Michel, et al. *Building United Judgment.* Madison, Wis.: Center for Conflict Resolution, 1981.

Bate, Paul and Mangham, Iain. *Exploring Participation.* New York: John Wiley and Sons, 1981.

Bean, Audrey. "Including the Supervisor in Employee Involvement Efforts." *National Productivity Review* (Winter 1986): 64-77.

Beck, Gustav. "The Men of Antigonish." *Journal of Adult Education* 7, 2 (1935).

Belman, Dale. "Unions, the Quality of Labor Relations, and Firm Performance." in *Unions and Economic Competitiveness.* Armonk, N.Y.: M. E. Sharpe, 1992.

Bennis, Warren G., Benne, Kenneth D., and Chin, Robert. *The Planning of*

Change. Fort Worth Tex.: Holt Rinehart and Winston, 1976.

Bernstein, Paul. *Workplace Democratization: Its Internal Dynamics.* Kent, Ohio: Kent State University Press, 1976.

Bester, Arthur, et al. "Democracy in Crisis." *Journal of Adult Education* 13, 3 (1941).

Bixler, Bob. "Empowered Measurement Systems: Catalyst for Improvement." *Tapping the Network Journal* (Summer 1993) 17-21.

Blumberg, Paul. *Industrial Democracy: The Sociology of Participation.* London: Constable and Co. Ltd., 1968.

Boone, Edgar J. *Developing Programs In Adult Education.* Englewood Cliffs, N.J.: Prentice-Hall, 1985.

Bradford, Leland P. and Lippitt, Ronald. "Building a Democratic Work Group." *Personnel* 22, 3 (1945).

Brookfield, Stephen, ed. *Learning Democracy: Eduard Lindeman on Adult Education and Social Change.* London: Croom Helm, 1987.

Brookfield, Stephen. *Developing Critical Thinkers.* San Francisco: Jossey-Bass, 1990.

Brown, Mark Graham. *Baldrige Award Winning Quality.* New York: Quality Resources Press, 1996.

Byham, W.C. and Cox, Jeff. *Zapp!: The Lightning of Empowerment.* New York: Harmony, 1988.

Camens, Sam. "Greater Industrial Democracy" in *Participative Systems at Work.* ed. Sidney Rubenstein. New York: Human Sciences Press, 1987.

Campbell, Alastair. *The Democratic Control of Work.* Oxford: Plunkett Foundation for Co-operative Studies, 1987.

Carnoy, Martin. "Education, Industrial Democracy and the State." *Economic and Industrial Democracy* (May 1981): 243-260.

Chell, Liz and Fielden, Derrick. "Achieving Industrial Democracy via Non-Formal Education." *Employee Relations* (1980).

Clark, Jennifer. "Empowerment Within." *Tapping the Network Journal* (Spring 1993) 14-17.

Clark, Peter. *Organizational Design.* London: Tavistock Press, 1972.

Clegg, Hugh. *Industrial Democracy and Nationalization.* Oxford: Basil Blackwell Publisher, 1951.

Coady, Moses. *Masters of Their Own Destiny.* New York: Harper and Brothers, 1939.

Coates, Ken and Topham, Tony. *Workers' Control.* London: Panther Modern Society Books, 1970.

Coch, Lester and French, John. "Overcoming Resistance to Change." *Human Relations* (1948): 512-532.

Cohen-Rosenthal, Edward. "Orienting Labor-Management Cooperation toward Revenue and Growth." *National Productivity Review* (Autumn 1985): 385-396.

Cohen-Rosenthal, Edward and Burton, Cynthia. "Improving Organizational Quality by Forging the Best Union-Management Relationship." *National Pro-*

ductivity Review (Spring 1994): 215-231.

Coit, Eleanor. "Worker's Education and Government Support." *Journal of Adult Education* 8, 3 (1936).

Cole, G. D. H. *The Case for Industrial Partnership.* London: MacMillan, 1957.

Cooper, Gary. *Group Training for Individual and Organizational Development.* Basel, Switzerland: S. Karger, 1972.

Cordery, John and Wall, Toby. "Work Design and Supervisory Practice." *Human Relations* (1985): 425-441.

Covey, Stephen R. *The 7 Habits of Highly Effective People.* New York: Simon and Shuster, 1989.

Daloz, Laurent A. *Effective Teaching and Mentoring.* San Francisco: Jossey-Bass, 1987.

Davis, Philip A. "Building a Workable Participative Management System." *Management Review* (March 1981): 26-39.

Davis, Rob. "Employee Empowerment at AT&T Universal Card Services." *Tapping the Network Journal* (Spring 1993): 10-11.

Deming, W. Edwards. *Out of the Crisis.* Cambridge: Massachusetts Institute of Technology, 1986.

Denison, Daniel. "Sociotechnical Design and Self-Managing Work Groups." *Journal of Occupational Behavior* (October 1982): 297-314.

Derber, Milton. *The American Idea of Industrial Democracy, 1865-1965.* Urbana: University of Illinois Press, 1970.

de Schweinitz, Dorothea. *Labor and Management in a Common Enterprise.* Cambridge: Harvard University Press, 1949.

Dew, John R. "The Critical Role of Auditing in Continuous Improvement." *National Productivity Review* 13, 3 (Summer 1994): 417-422.

Dew, John R. "Creating Team Leaders" *The Journal for Quality and Participation* 18, 6 (October 1995): 50-54.

Dewey, John. *Democracy and Education.* New York: MacMillan Free Press, 1916.

DeWitt, Sherri. *Worker Participation and the Crisis of Liberal Democracy.* Boulder, Colo.: Westview Press, 1980.

Drulovic, Milojko. *Self-Management On Trial.* Bristol England: Spokesman Books, 1978.

Dumaine, Brian. "Who Needs a Boss?" *Quality Digest (June 1990): 53-64.*

Dunn, John. *Democracy: The Unfinished Journey.* Oxford: Oxford University Press, 1992.

Dutton, Barbara. "Employee Involvement: How It works." *Quality Digest* (June 1989): 46-55.

Elden, Max. "Democratizing Organizations: A Challenge to Organization Development." in *Human Systems Development.* ed. Robert Tannenbaum. San Francisco: Jossey-Bass, 1987.

Emery, Fred and Thorsrud, Einar. *Democracy at Work.* Leiden: Martinus Nijhoff, 1976.

Faris, Nadir. "Employees Design Site Recognition System." *Tapping the Network*

Journal (Spring 1993): 18-22.

Fendt, Paul F. and Vavrek, G. Michael, eds. *Quality Improvement In Continuing and Higher Education and Service Organizations.* Lewiston: The Edwin Mellen Press, 1992.

Fisher, Roger and Ury, William. *Getting to Yes.* New York: Penguin Books, 1981.

Fleming, Michael. "Entergy Turns the Corner in Total Quality Implementation with Natural Work Teams." *Tapping the Network Journal.* (Summer 1994): 13-18.

Follett, Mary Parker. *Dynamic Administration.* New York: Harper and Brothers, 1942.

Frank, Glenn. "On the Firing Line of Democracy." *Journal of Adult Education (Febraury 1929).*

Freire, Paulo. *The Politics of Education.* South Hadley, Mass: Bergin & Garvey, 1985.

Furtado, Thomas. "Training for a Different Management Style" *Personnel Management (March 1988): 40-43.*

Galagan, Patricia. "Work Teams That Work." *Training and Development Journal* (November 1986): 33-35.

Gantt, Henry. *Industrial Leadership.* New Haven: Yale University Press, 1916.

Gills, Barry, et al. *Low Intensity Democracy.* London: Pluto Press, 1993.

Gold, Charlotte. *Labor Management Committees.* Ithaca, N.Y.: ILR Press, 1986.

Gompers, Samuel. *Labor and the Employer.* New York: E.P. Dutton, 1920.

Gonnodo, Bill. "Employee Involvement: How It Works In Motorola's National Service Division." *Quality Digest* (September 1989): 40-47.

Goodman, Paul. *Designing Effective Work Groups.* San Francisco: Jossey-Bass, 1986.

Graham-Moore, Brian and Ross, Timothy L. *Gainsharing: Plans for Improving Performance.* Washington, D.C.: Bureau of National Affairs, 1990.

Grazier, Peter. *Before It's Too Late.* Chadds Ford, Pa.: Teambuilding Inc., 1989.

Griffin, Donna S. "Making a Measurable Difference Through Empowerment." *Tapping the Network Journal* (Summer 1993): 2-4.

Guillory, William A. *Realizations: Personal Empowerment Through Self-Awareness.* Salt Lake City, Utah: Innovations Publishing, 1985.

Gunn, Christopher. *Worker's Self-Management in the United States.* Ithaca, N.Y.: Cornell University Press, 1984.

Hammer, Michael and Champy, James. *Reengineering the Corporation.* New York: Harper, 1993.

Hammerstone, James and Barley, Gilbert. "Lessons Learned in Setting Up Work Teams." *Tapping the Network Journal* (Spring 1990): 7-11.

Heron, John. *The Facilitators' Handbook.* London: Kogan Page Ltd., 1989.

Hewitt, Dorothy. *Adult Education: A Dynamic for Democracy.* New York: Appleton-Century Co., 1937.

Hicks, Robert F. and Bone, Diane. *Self-Managing Teams.* Los Altos Calif: Crisp Publications, 1990.

Hinckley, Stanley. "A Closer Look at Participation." *Organizational Dynamics* (1985): 57-67.

Hordes, Mark. "The Power of Participative Management: Steps to Success." *Notebook* (December 1989): 1-4.

Horton, Myles and Freire, Paulo. *We Make the Road by Walking.* Philadelphia: Temple University Press, 1990.

Hunnuis, Gerry. et al. *Worker's Control.* New York: Vintage Books, 1973.

Hurst, P.G. *Autonomous Group Functioning.* London: Tavistock Publications, 1962.

I Speak Your Language. New York: DBM Publishing, 1994.

IDE Group. *Industrial Democracy in Europe, Oxford: Clarendon Press, 1981.*

Ishikawa, Kaoru. *Guide to Quality Control.* Tokyo: Asian Productivity Organization, 1982.

Jackson, Tom. "Forging the Workteam: Beyond Quality Circles." *National Productivity Review* (Spring 1982): 192-203.

Janis, Irving. *Victims of Group Think.* Boston: Houghton Miffin Co., 1972.

Jarvis, Peter, ed. *Twentieth Century Thinkers In Adult Education.* London: Croom Helm, 1987.

Johansen, Bruce E. *Forgotten Founders.* Boston: Harvard Common Press, 1982.

Juran, Joseph. *Managerial Breakthrough.* New York: McGraw-Hill, 1964.

Kanter, Rosabeth Moss. "The New Workforce Meets the Changing Workplace: Strains Dilemmas, and Contradictions in Attempts to Implement Participative and Entrepreneurial Management." *Human Resources Management* (Winter 1986): 515-537.

Kepner, Benjamin and Tregoe, Charles. *The New Rational Manager.* Princeton, N.J.: Princeton Research Press, 1981.

Keppler, Robert. "What the Supervisor Should Know about Participative Management." *Supervisory Management* (May 1978): 34-40.

Klein, Gerald. "Employee Centered Productivity and QWL Programs." *National Productivity Review* (Autumn 1986): 348-362.

Klein, Janice. "Why Supervisors Resist Employee Involvement." *Harvard Business Review* (September 1984): 87-95.

Knowles, Malcolm. *The Modern Practice of Adult Education.* New York: Cambridge Press, 1984.

Knowles, Malcolm and Knowles, Hulda. *Introduction to Group Dynamics.* New York: Follett Publishing, 1972.

Kochanski, James. "Hiring in Self-Regulating Teams." *National Productivity Review* (Spring 1987): 153-159.

Kolaja, Jiri. *Workers' Councils.* New York: Frederick A Praeger, 1965.

Krimerman, Len, ed. *When Workers Decide.* Philadelphia: New Society Publishers, 1992.

Kroeger, Otto and Thuesen, Janet M. *Type Talk at Work.* New York: Delacorte Press, 1992.

LaMonica, Elaine L. *Lamonica Empathy Profile.* Tuxedo, N.Y.: XICOM, 1986.

Lather, Patti. "Research as Praxis." *Harvard Educational Review* (August 1986):

257-277.

Lauck, W. Jett. *Political and Industrial Democracy:* 1776-1926. New York: Funk and Wagnalls, 1926.

Lawler, Edward. *High Involvement Management.* San Francisco: Jossey-Bass, 1988.

Lawler, Edward. "Substitutes for Hiearchy." *Organizational Dynamics* (Summer 1988): 5-15.

Lazes, Peter and Costanza, Tony. "Cutting Costs without Layoffs through Union-Management Collaboration." *National Productivity Review* (Autumn 1983): 362-370.

Lazes, Peter, et al. "Xerox and the ACTWU: Using Labor-Management Teams to Remain Competitive." *National Productivity Review* (Summer 1991): 339-349.

Leana, Carrie. "Power Relinquishment Versus Power Sharing: Theoretical Clarification and Empirical Comparison of Delegation and Participation." *Journal of Applied Psychology* (1987): 228-233.

Lee, Chris. "Beyond Teamwork." *Quality Digest* (August 1990): 20-39.

Lewin, David. "Collective Bargaining and the Quality of Work Life" *Organizational Dynamics (Autumn 1981): 37-53.*

Lewin, Kurt. "The Practicality of Democracy." *Human Nature and Enduring Peace.* Boston: Houghton-Mifflin Co., 1945.

Likert, Rensis. *New Patterns of Management.* New York: McGraw-Hill, 1961.

Lindeman, Eduard. *The Democratic Man.* Boston: Beacon Press, 1956.

Locke, Edwin, et al. "Participation in Decision Making: When Should It Be Used?" *Organizational Dynamics (Winter 1986): 65-79.*

London, Manuel. *Change Agents.* San Francisco: Jossey-Bass, 1990.

Long, Huey B. and Lawry, Constance. "Fannia Mary Cohn: An educational leader in labor and worker's education, her life and times." in *Breaking New Ground: The Development of Adult and Worker's Education in North America.* ed. Huey Long. Syracuse, N.Y.: Syracuse University Press, 1990.

Lovrich, Nicholas. "The Dangers of Participative Management." *Review of Public Personnel Administration* (Summer 1985): 9-25.

Mandl, Vladimir. "Teaming Up for Performance." *Quality Digest* (September 1990): 42-53.

Mangiapane, Adele. "Empowering People to Improve a Process." *Quality Digest* (June 1988): 60-71.

Mann, Charles. "Self-Discipline In a Democracy." *Journal of Adult Education* 13, 3 (1941).

Manz, Charles, et al. "Preparing for an Organizational Change to Employee Self-Management." *Organizational Dynamics* (1990).

Marchington, Mick. *Responses to Participation at Work.* Westmead, England: Gower Press, 1980.

Marrow, Alfred. *Management by Participation.* New York: Harper and Row, 1967.

Marsick, Victoria J. "Action Learning and Reflection in the Workplace." in *Fostering Critical Reflection in Adulthood.* ed. Jack Mezirow. San Francisco: Jossey-

Bass, 1990.

Martin, Everett. "The Dangers of Democracy." *Journal of Adult Education* 7, 3 (1935).

Mayo, Elton. *The Social Problems of an Industrial Civilization.* Andover, Mass.: Andover Press, 1945.

McMurry, Robert. "The Case for Benevolent Autocracy." *Harvard Business Review* (1958): 82-90.

Meyer, Christopher. "How the Right Measures Help Teams Excel." *Harvard Business Review* (May-June 1994): 95-103.

Mezirow, Jack. *Fostering Critical Reflection in Adulthood.* San Francisco: Jossey-Bass, 1990.

Mhetras, V.G. *Labour Participation in Management.* Bombay: Manataktalas Books, 1966.

Miller, Lawrence. "Creating the New High-Commitment Culture." *Supervisory Management* (August 1985): 21-28.

Mishel, Lawrence and Voos, Paula B. *Unions and Economic Competitiveness.* Armonk, N.Y.: Economic Policy Institute, 1992.

Mohrman, Sue. "Empowerment: There's More to It Than Meets the Eye." *Tapping the Network Journal* (Spring 1993): 14-17.

Mosley, Donald C. "Nominal Grouping As an Organization Development Intervention Technique." *Training and Development Journal* (March 1974): 30-37.

Naisbitt, John. *Global Paradox.* New York: Avon Books, 1994.

Nakajima, Seiichi. "Revitalization of Small Group Activities." *The International QC Forum.* (May 1986), 63-73.

Olson, Magarethe. *Technological Support for Work Group Collaboration.* Hillsdale, N.J.: Lawrence Erlbaum Associates, 1989.

Orpen, Christopher. "Management Attitudes to Industrial Democracy." *Management International Review* (1980): 111-125.

Orsburn, Jack D. *Self-Directed Work Teams: The New American Challenge.* Homewood, Il.: Richard Irwin Inc., 1990.

Parker, Glenn M. *Team Players and Teamwork: The New Competitive Business Strategy.* San Francisco: Jossey-Bass, 1990.

Parry, Scott B. *From Managing to Empowering.* New York: Quality Resources Press, 1994.

Pasmore, William. "Overcoming the Roadblocks to Work-Restructuring Efforts." *Organizational Dynamics* (Spring 1982): 54-67.

Pasmore, William. *Designing Effective Organizations.* New York: John Wiley and Sons, 1988.

Pell, Orlie. "Jobs in Workers Education." *Adult Education Journal* (1950): 9, No. 2.

Pierce, Richard. *Involvement Engineering.* Milwaukee: ASQC Press, 1986.

Pilsworth, Michael and Ruddock, Ralph. "Persons, Not Respondents: Alternative Approach in the Study of Social Processes." in *Creating Knowledge: A Monopoly?* 1988.

Prince, George M. "Creative Meetings Through Power Sharing." *Harvard Business Review* (1972): 50, No. 4.

Rhenman, Eric. *Industrial Democracy and Industrial Management.* London: Tavistock Press, 1968.

Richardson, Peter. "Courting Greater Employee Involvement through Participative Management." *Sloan Management Review* (Winter 1985): 33-44.

Rienstra, John A. "Empowering a Team to Revamp the Suggestion System." *Tapping the Network Journal* (Spring 1993): 8-9.

Riggan, Diane. "What Labor and Management Can Do About the Sad State of Cooperative Efforts." *A Brief. Houston, Tx.: American Productivity and Quality Center* (February 1989).

Roberts, Ernie. *Workers' Control.* London: Allen and Unwin Ltd., 1973.

Rogers, Carl. *On Becoming a Person.* Boston: Houghton Mifflin Co., 1961.

Rosenbaum, Mark. "Partners in Productivity: An Emerging Consensus in Labor-Management Relations." *National Productivity Review* (Autumn 1989): 357-364.

Rosow, Jerome and Zager, Robert. *New Roles for Managers.* Scarsdale, N.Y.: Work in America Institute, 1989.

Ross, Timothy. "Employee Involvement and the Perils of Democracy." *National Productivity Review* (Autumn 1987): 348-357.

Rothstein, Lawrence. "The Empowerment Effort That Came Undone." *Harvard Business Review* (January-February 1995): 20-31.

Rubinstein, Sidney. *Participative Systems at Work.* New York: Human Sciences Press, Inc., 1987.

Sanderson, George. *Industrial Democracy Today.* Toronto: McGraw-Hill, 1979.

Sashkin, Marshall. "Participative Management Remains an Ethical Imperative." *Organizational Dynamics* (1985), 62-74.

Scholtes, Peter R. *The Team Handbook.* Madison, Wis.: Joiner Associates, 1988.

Schon, Donald A. *The Reflective Practitioner.* New York: Basic Books, 1983.

Schuller, Tom. *Democracy at Work.* Oxford: Oxford University Press, 1985.

Scott, Cynthia and Jaffe, Dennis. *Empowerment.* Los Altos, Ca.: Crisp Publications, 1991.

Selekman, Ben. *Employes' Representation in Steel Works.* New York: Russell Sage Foundation, 1924.

Shonk, James. *Team-Based Organizations: Developing a Successful Team Environment.* Homewood, Il.: Business One Irwin, 1992.

Shor, Ira. *Empowering Education.* Chicago: University of Chicago Press, 1992.

Shuster, David. *Teaming For Quality Improvement.* Englewood Cliffs, N.J.: Prentice-Hall, 1990.

Simmons, John. "Participatory Management: Lessons From the Leaders." *Management Review* (December 1990): 54-58.

Simmons, Robert. "Control In an Age of Empowerment." *Harvard Business Review* (March-April 1995): 80-88.

Simpson, Eugene L. "Motorola's Participative Management Program." *Nation-*

al Productivity Review (Winter 1982): 56-62.

Sims, Henry and Manz, Charles C. "Conversations within Self-Managed Work Groups." *National Productivity Review* (Summer 1982): 261-269.

Sink, Scott, et al. "Performance Action Teams." *National Productivity Review* (1986): 233-251.

Somers, Ken. "Defining the Boundaries of Empowerment." *Tapping the Network Journal* (Spring 1993): 3-7.

Spiro, Herbert. *The Politics of German Codetermination.* Cambridge: Harvard University Press, 1958.

Stein, Barry and Kanter, Rosabeth Moss. "Building the Parallel Organization." *Journal of Applied Behavioral Science* (Fall 1980): 371-388.

Sundstrom, Eric, et al. "Work Teams: Applications and Effectiveness." *American Psychologist* (February 1990): 120-133.

Susman, G.I., et al. "The Scientific Merits of Action Research." *Administrative Science Quarterly* (1978): 578-590.

Tandon, Rajesh. *Creating Knowledge: A Monopoly?, 1988.*

Tannenbaum, Robert and Schmidt, Warren H. "How to Choose a Leadership Pattern." *Harvard Business Review* (March-April 1958).

Thomas, Kenneth and Kilmann, Ralph. *Thomas-Kilman Conflict Mode Instrument.* Tuxedo, N.Y.: XICOM, 1974.

Thor, Carl. "A Complete Organization Measurement System." *International Productivity Journal* (Spring 1990): 21-26.

Tjosvold, Dean. *Working Together to get Things Done.* Lexington, Mass.: Lexington Books, 1986.

Torres, Cresencio and Spiegal, Jerry. *Self-Directed Work Teams.* San Diego, Ca.: Pfeiffer, 1990.

Tregoe, Benjamin and Zimmerman, John W. *Top Management Strategy.* New York: Simon and Shuster, 1980.

Trist, Eric L., et al. *Organizational Change.* London: Tavistock Press, 1963.

Turner, Robert and Count, Roger. "Education for Industrial Democracy." *Economic and Industrial Democracy* (August 1981): 371-391.

Verespej, Michael. "When You Put the Team in Charge." *Industry Week* (December 3, 1990): 30-32.

Viklund, Birger. "Education for Participation." *The Labour Gazette* (September 1977): 390-391.

Vogt, Judith and Murrell, Kenneth. *Empowerment in Organizations.* San Diego, Ca.: University Associates, 1990.

Vroom, Victor and Yetton, Phillip. *Leadership and Decision Making.* Pittsburg, Pa.: University of Pittsburg Press, 1973.

Walling, William. *American Labor and American Democracy.* New York: Harper and Brothers, 1926.

Walton, Richard. "Do Supervisors Thrive in Participative Work Systems?" *Organizational Dynamics (Winter 1979): 25-38.*

Weisbord, Marvin. *Productive Workplaces.* San Francisco: Jossey-Bass, 1987.

Weisbord, Marvin. *Discovering Common Ground.* San Francisco: Barrett Koehler Publishers, 1992.

Whyte, William F. *Pattern for Industrial Peace.* New York: Harper Brothers, 1951.

Whyte, William F. *Men at Work.* Homewood, Ill.: Dorsey Press, 1961.

Whyte, William F. *Worker Participation and Ownership.* Ithaca, N.Y.: ILR Press, 1983.

Whyte, William F. *Making Mandragon.* Ithaca, N.Y.: Cornell University Press, 1988.

Wilson, H.B. *Democracy and the Work Place.* Montreal: Black Rose Books, 1974.

Wilson, Robert and Melrose, Julie. "Making a Difference: Employee Participation in Massachusetts." *Quality Digest* (February 1988): 30-38.

Wirth, Arther. "Issues Affecting Education and Work in the Eighties." *Teachers College Record* (September 1977): 55-67.

Witte, John F. *Democracy, Authority, and Alienation In Work.* Chicago: University of Chicago Press, 1980.

Xenophon. *Anabasis.* Cambridge: Harvard University Press, 1922.

Zwerdling, Daniel. *Workplace Democracy.* New York: Harper and Row, 1978.

Index

About the Author

JOHN R. DEW is the Cost Reduction and Continuous Improvement Manager for Lockheed Martin Utility Services. Dr. Dew has over two decades of experience in Total Quality Management and training, and has published a number of articles on this subject.

ISBN 1-56720-094-X

EAN

9 781567 200942

HARDCOVER BAR CODE

90000>